I0568074

WELCOME

THIS BOOK BELONG TO :

....

Find Us On

Website www.adropfromeden.com

Instagram https://www.instagram.com/adropfromeden/

Twitter https://twitter.com/adropfromeden

Facebook aromatherapy group https://www.facebook.com/groups/adropfromeden

Facebook Ministry Group https://www.facebook.com/groups/adropfromedenministry

About The Author

Hello, God's children my name is Felicia Patterson, I hold a degree in psychology, aromatherapy as well as am an Ordained Minister. Journaling has helped me through some very tough times in my life along with my faith and I thought why not combine the two. I could go on about my accomplishments but instead, I would like to share with you a personal story of what the power of faith and prayer can do.

About The Author

I was born with a rare spinal condition. My parents reached out to all the greats, but all said there was no treatment and just keep me comfortable until my time came. After months of searching and praying, a young and brilliant neurosurgeon came up with a plan that would hopefully work. Prior to what was to be a series of surgeries, I wanted to see the Happy Hunters that were a few hours away from us. Things were tight but my parents made it happen but only had fifty dollars to travel on. We got to the motel got cleaned up and walked across the street where they were giving the sermon. At this time, I had lost all function of my lower extremities and I had to be carried into the church. Prior to the sermon, they were passing the plate. We only had enough to get back home, so we don't have anything to spare. As they were passing the plate my mom put the fifty dollars in. The lady minister whom I will never forget asked my dad to sit me beside her. While her husband was giving the sermon, she was rubbing my back. My parents had communicated with them through email, but she had no knowledge of who we were or my condition. After a while, she asked my mom and another woman to take my hands and walk me around the church. I had not walked in months yet practically ran around the church. After it was over, we were headed for the lobby when the same woman that walked with me around the church came up to my mom and said, "God told me to give you this" and gave her two twenties and a ten. Our Life is a testament that through all the challenges, loss, and despair that we must hold to our faith and trust that we are all here for a purpose.

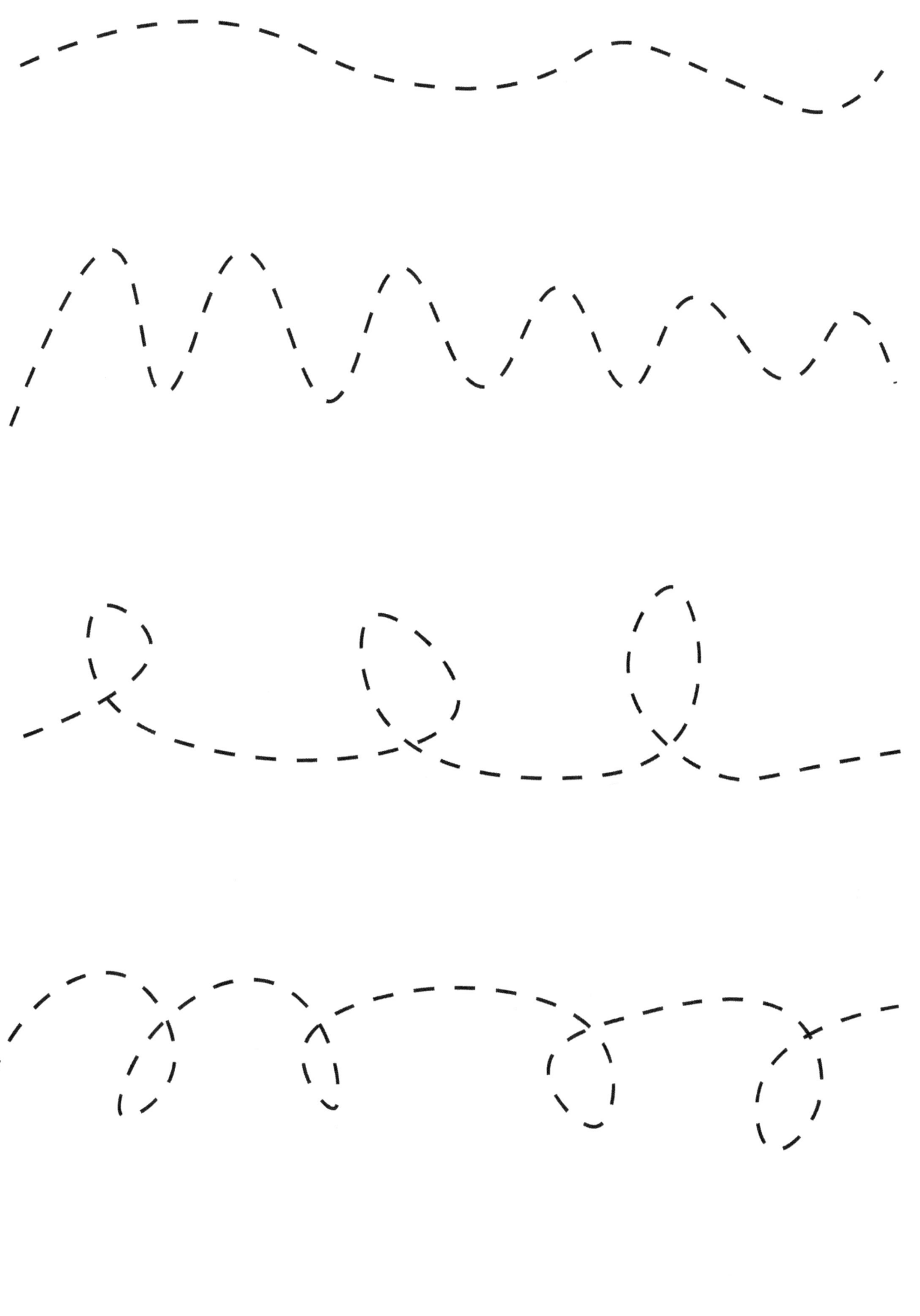

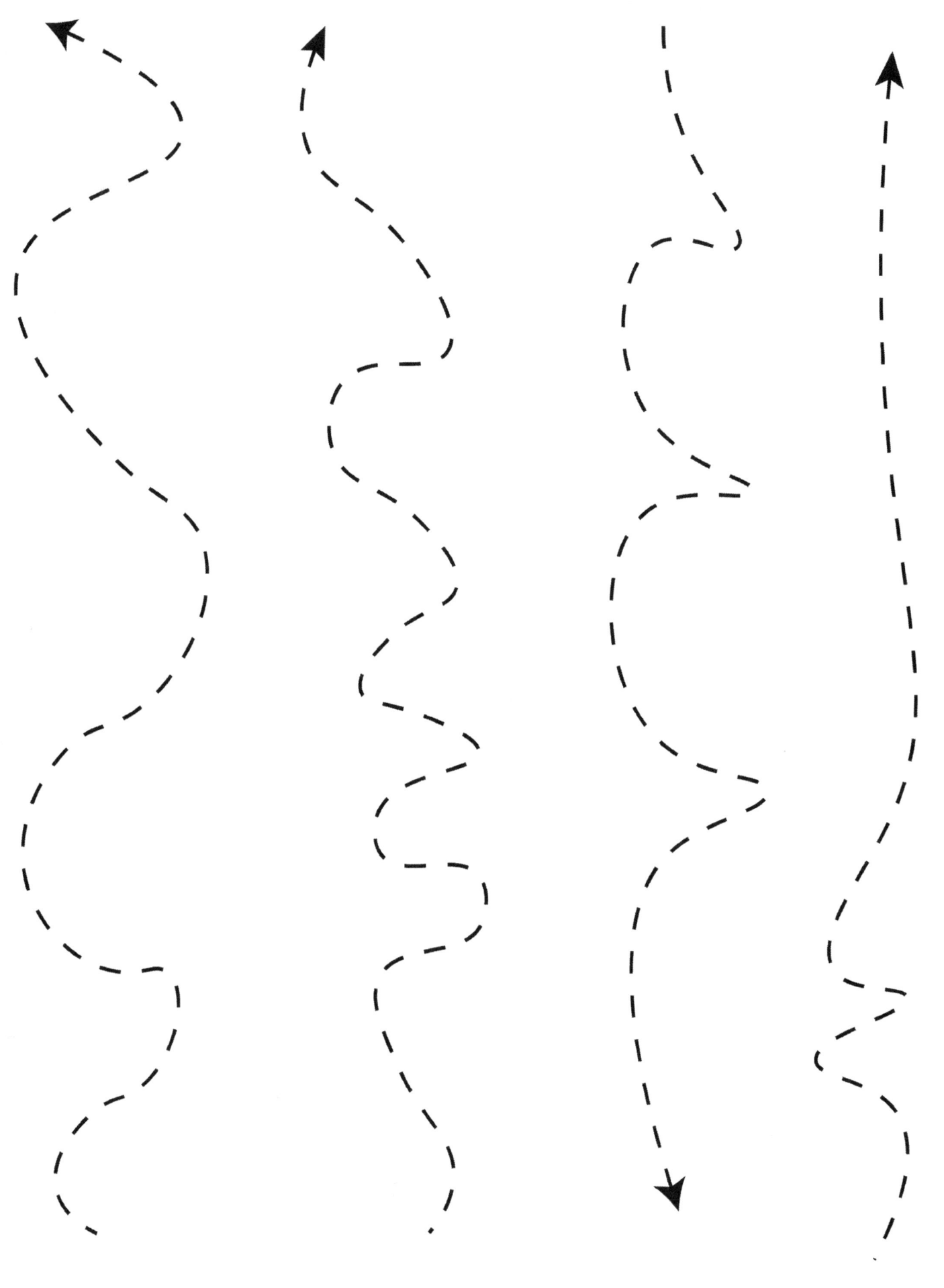

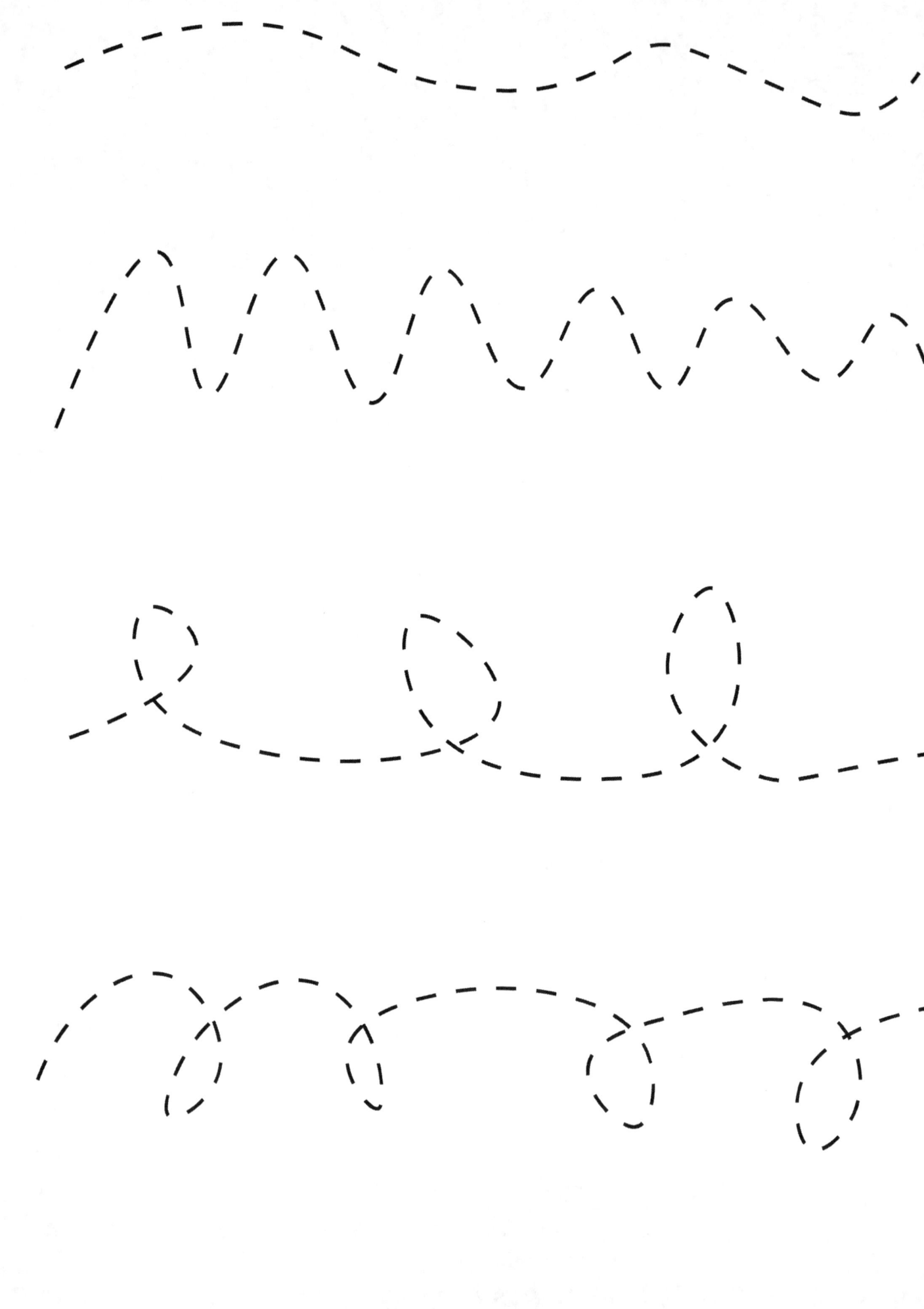

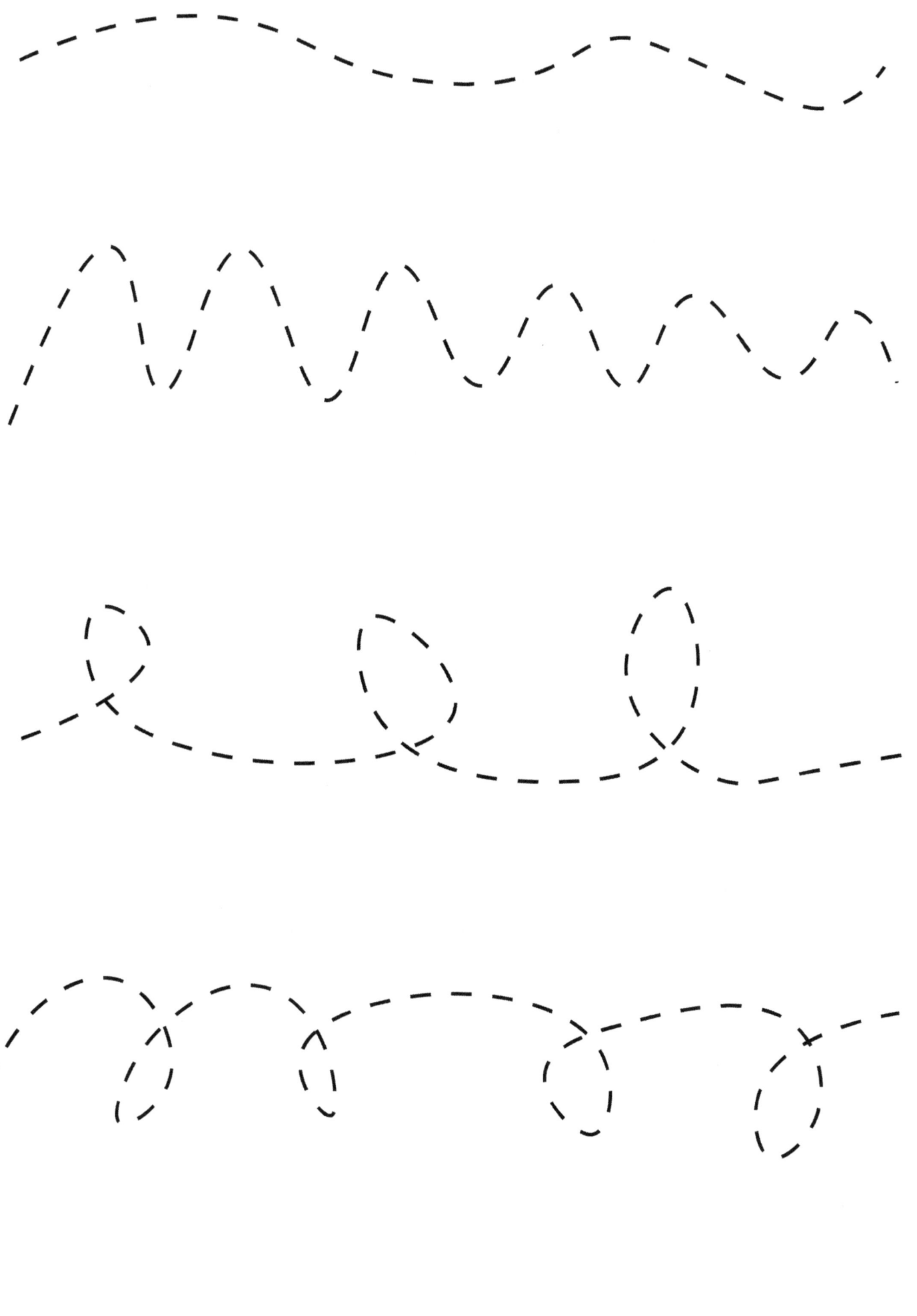

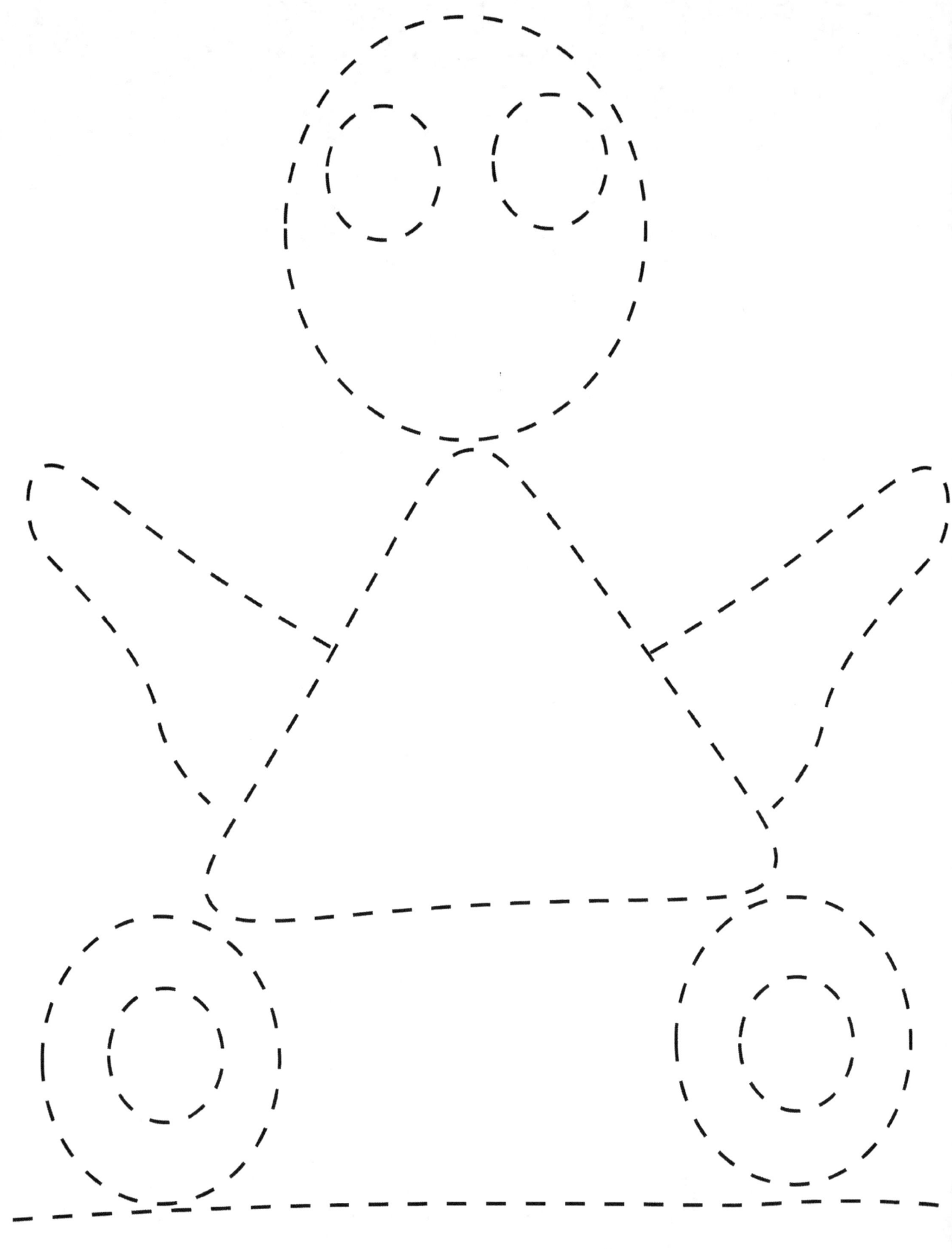

A for Ant

A → Axe	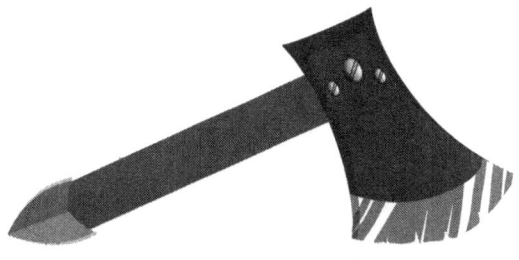
A → Apple	
A → Animale	

let,s to color

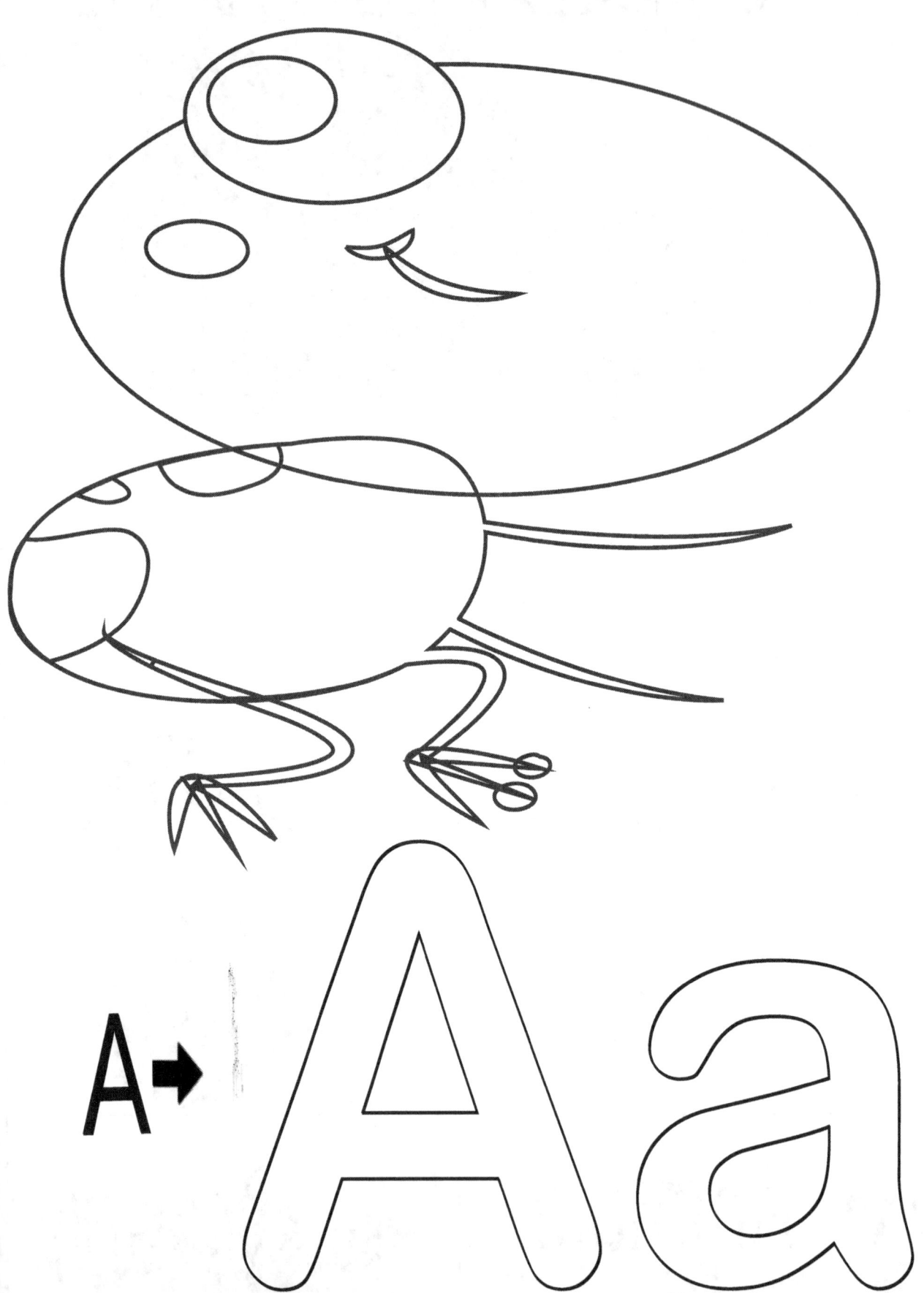

A→

Aa

A A A A A A

a a a a a a

A A A A A A

a a a a a a

A A A A A A

a a a a a a

A A A A A A

a a a a a a

B For Banana

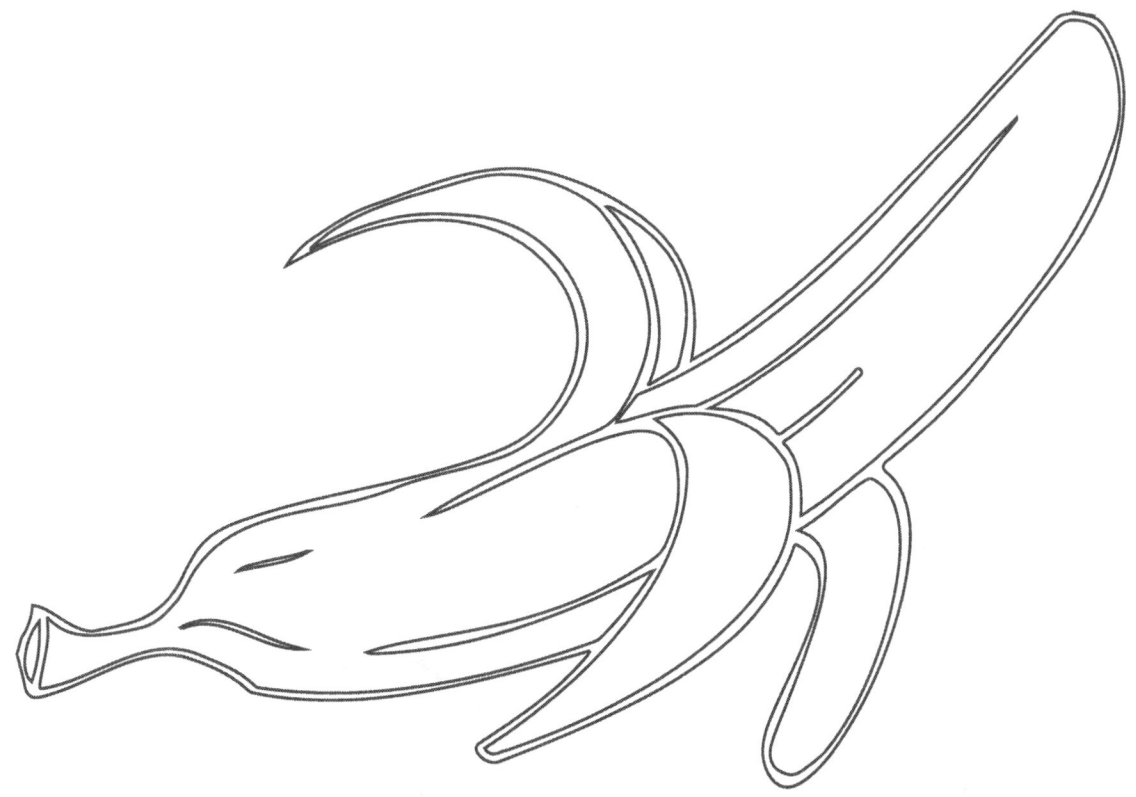

B ➜ Ball	
B ➜ Bananas	
B ➜ Bee	

let,s to color

B ➡ **Bb**

B b

B   B   B   B   B

b   b   b   b   b

B   B   B   B   B

b   b   b   b   b

B   B   B   B   B

b   b   b   b   b

B   B   B   B   B

b   b   b   b   b

C FOR CAT

C → Cow	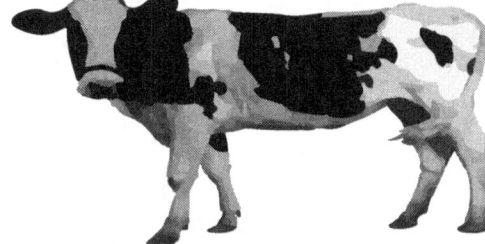
C → carrot	
C → Chicken	

let,s to color

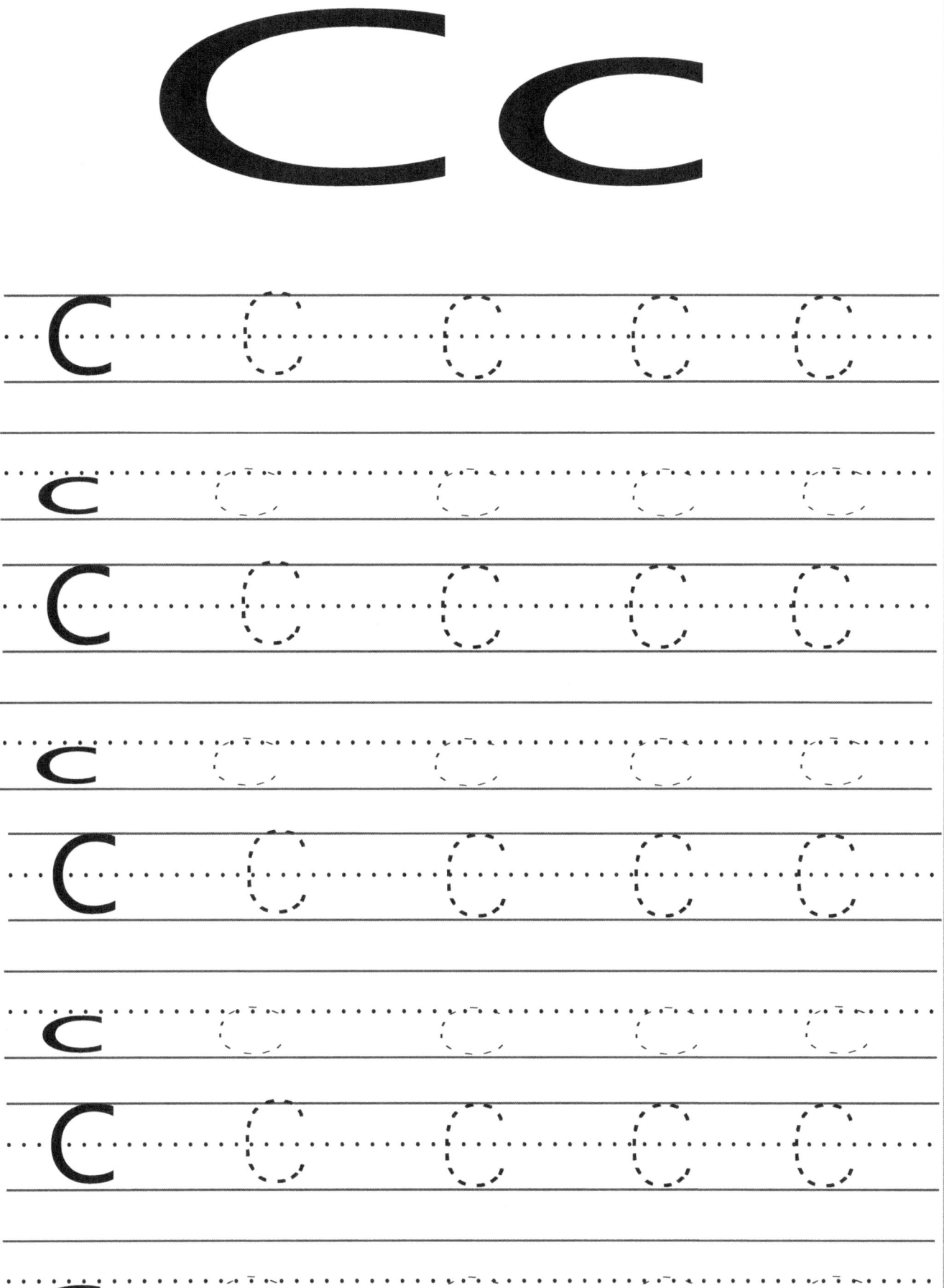

D FOR Duck

D → Dolphin	
D → Dinosaur	
D → Doll	

let,s to color

D ➔

D d

D · · · D · · · · · · · D · · · · · · · D · · · · · · · D · · ·

d · · · · d · · · · · · · d · · · · · · · d · · · · · · · d · · ·

D · · · D · · · · · · · D · · · · · · · D · · · · · · · D · · ·

d · · · · d · · · · · · · d · · · · · · · d · · · · · · · d · · ·

D · · · D · · · · · · · D · · · · · · · D · · · · · · · D · · ·

d · · · · d · · · · · · · d · · · · · · · d · · · · · · · d · · ·

D · · · D · · · · · · · D · · · · · · · D · · · · · · · D · · ·

d · · · · d · · · · · · · d · · · · · · · d · · · · · · · d · · ·

E FOR Elephent

E ▸ Eagle	
E ▸ Eye	
E ▸ Eggplant	

TO COLOR

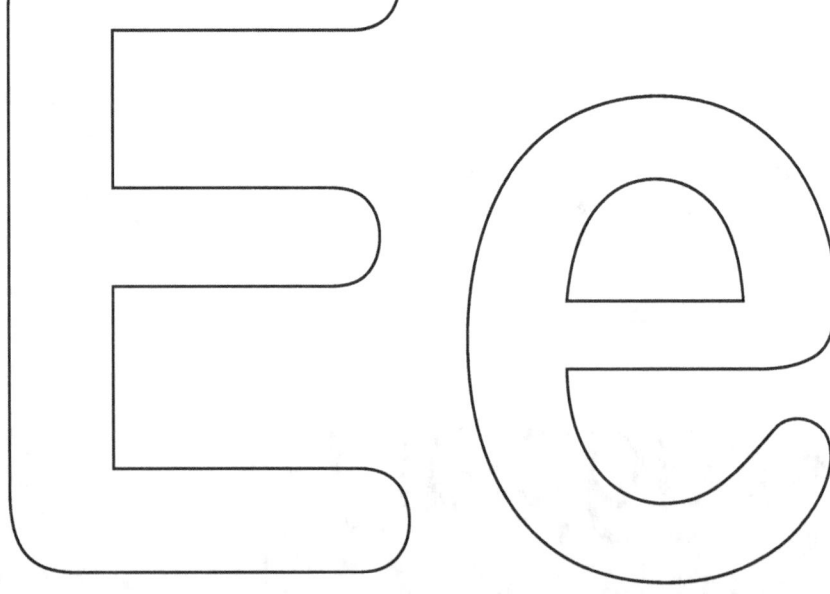

E ➡ Ee

E e

E · · · · · · · ⌐¬ · · · · · ⌐¬ · · · · · ⌐¬ · · · · · ⌐¬

e · · · · · · ◯ · · · · · ◯ · · · · · ◯ · · · · · ◯

E · · · · · · · ⌐¬ · · · · · ⌐¬ · · · · · ⌐¬ · · · · · ⌐¬

e · · · · · · ◯ · · · · · ◯ · · · · · ◯ · · · · · ◯

E · · · · · · · ⌐¬ · · · · · ⌐¬ · · · · · ⌐¬ · · · · · ⌐¬

e · · · · · · ◯ · · · · · ◯ · · · · · ◯ · · · · · ◯

E · · · · · · · ⌐¬ · · · · · ⌐¬ · · · · · ⌐¬ · · · · · ⌐¬

e · · · · · · ◯ · · · · · ◯ · · · · · ◯ · · · · · ◯

F FOR Frog

F → Fish	
F → Flower	
F → Fox	

let,s to color

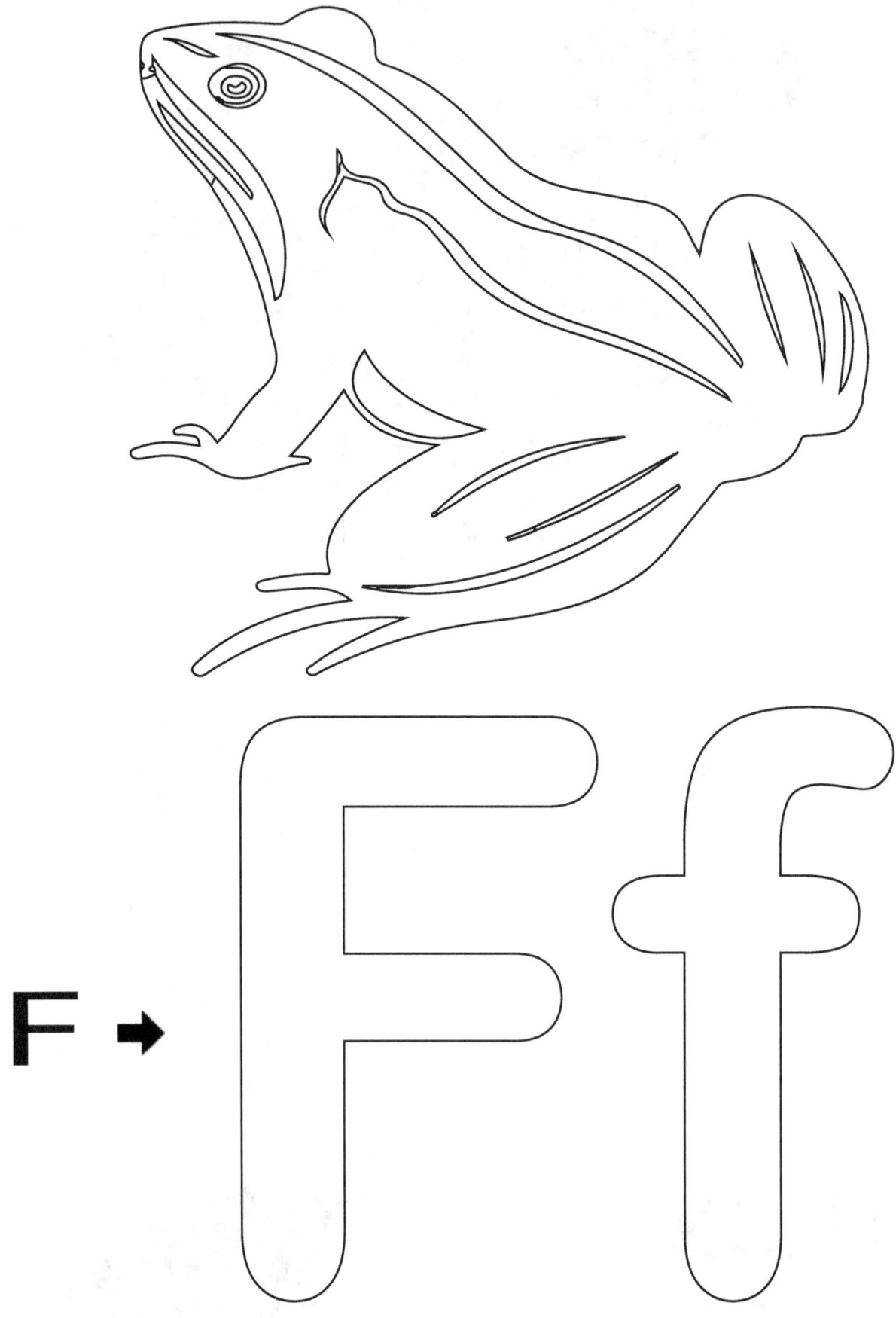

F ➤

F f

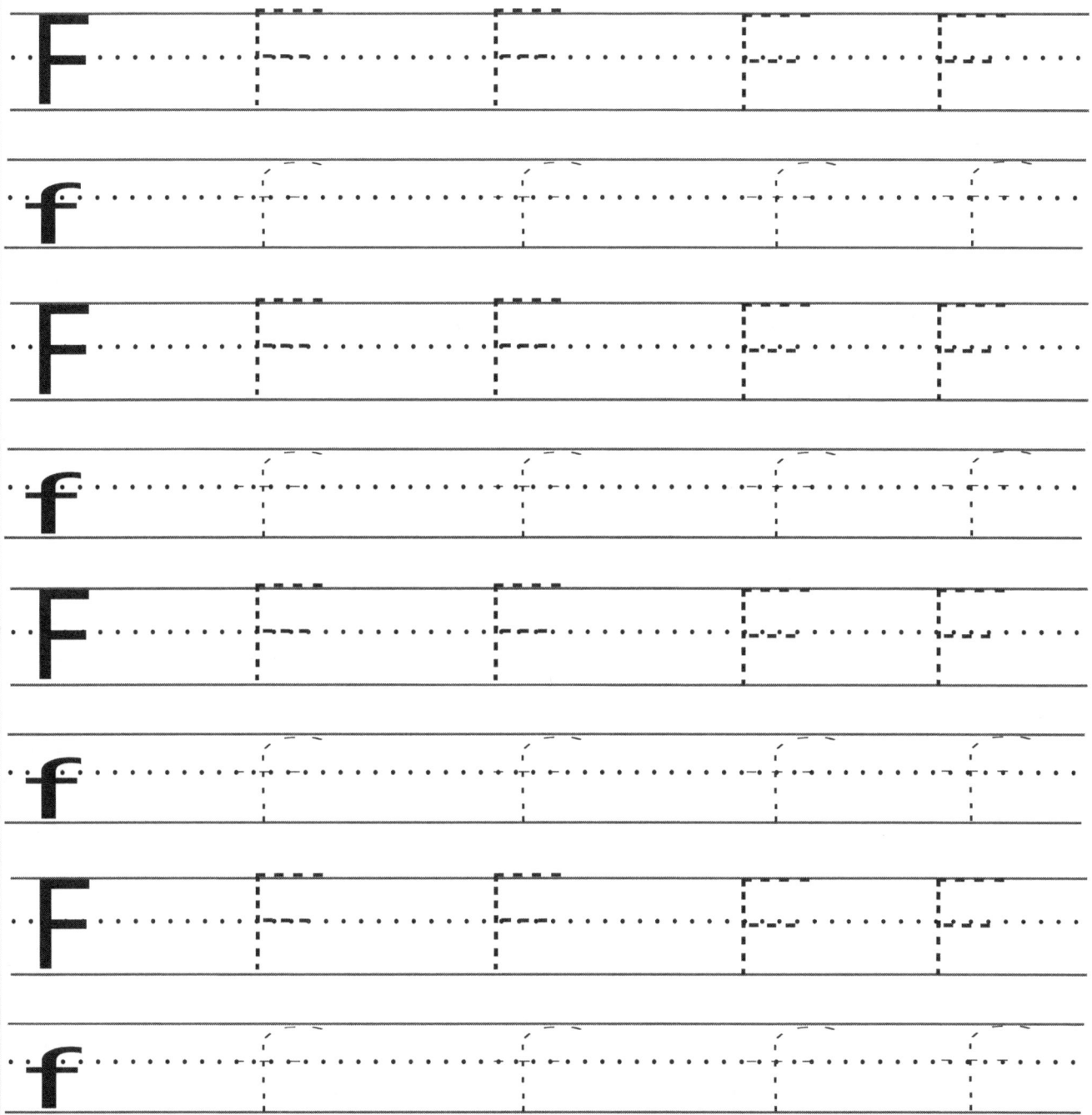

G For Goat

G ➜ Grapes	
G ➜ Gorilla	
G ➜ Guiter	

let,s to color

G ➔ Gg

G g

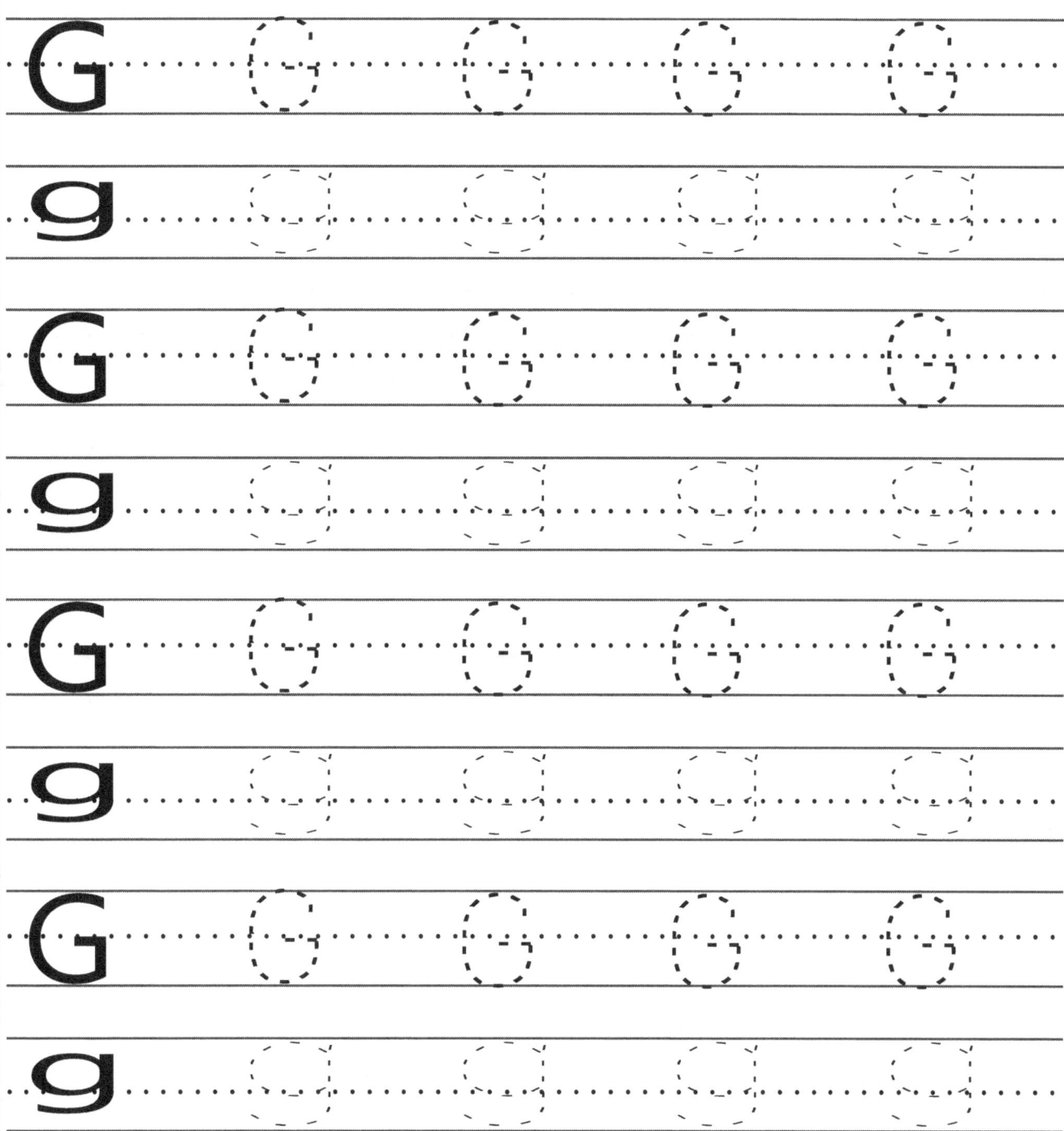

H FOR Helicopter

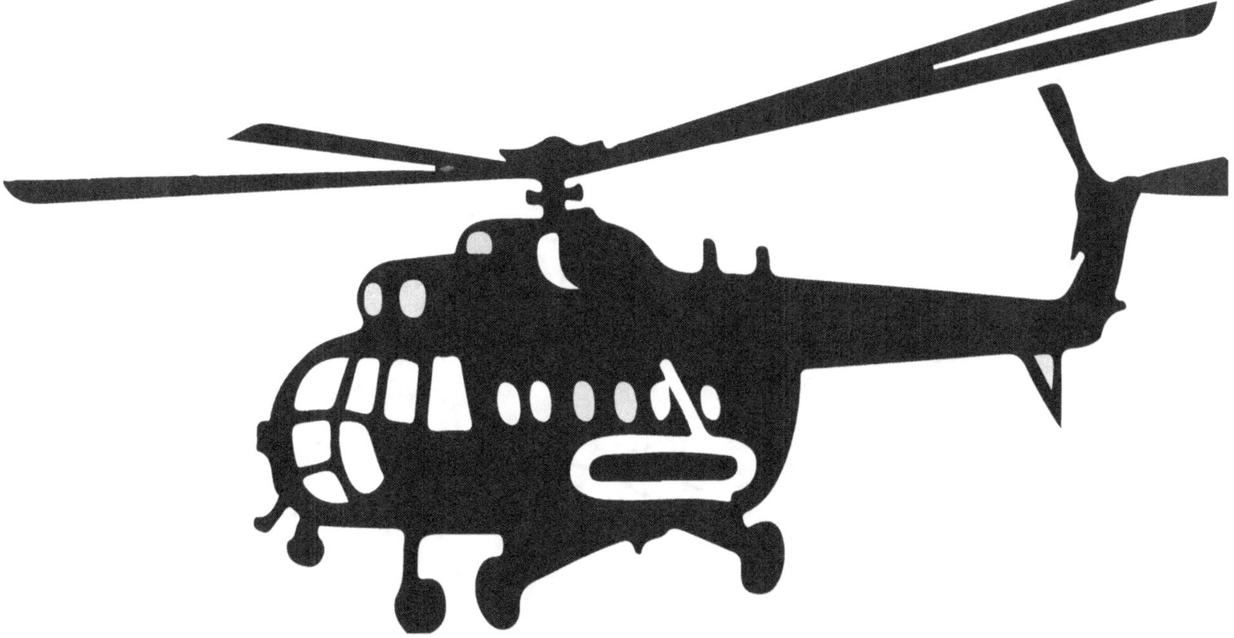

H → Home	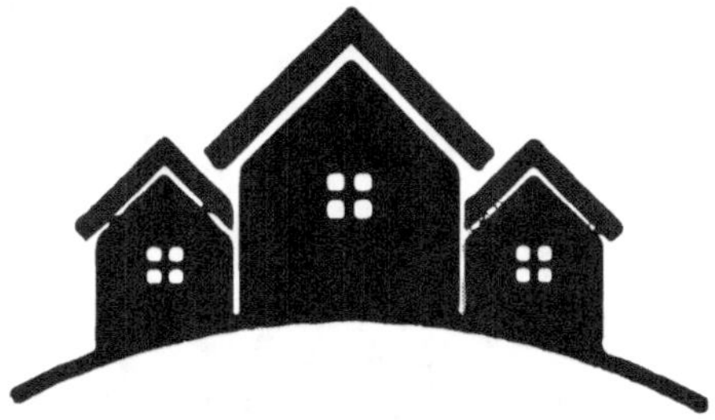
H → Hat	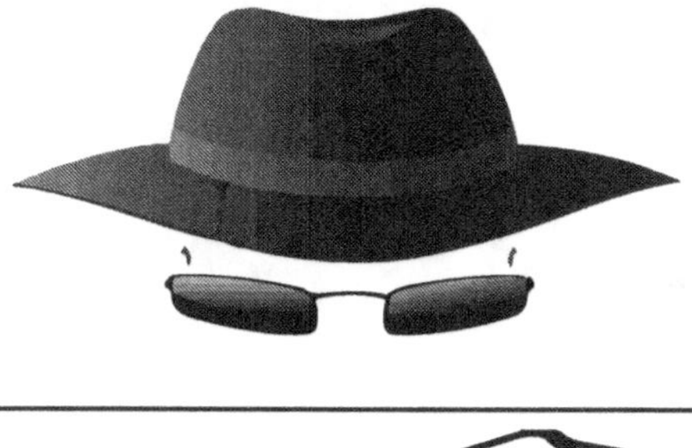
H → Harmonica	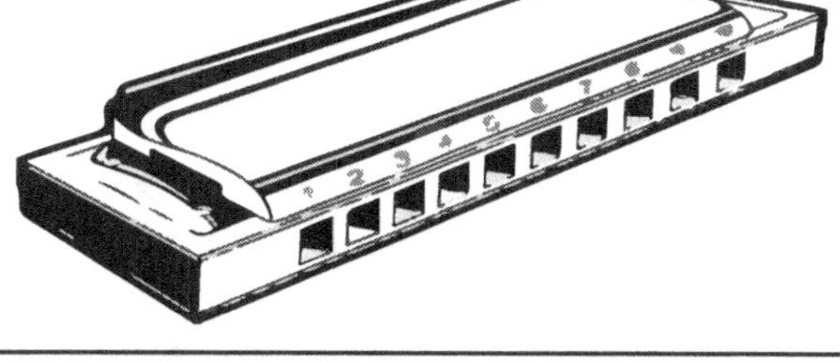

let,s to color

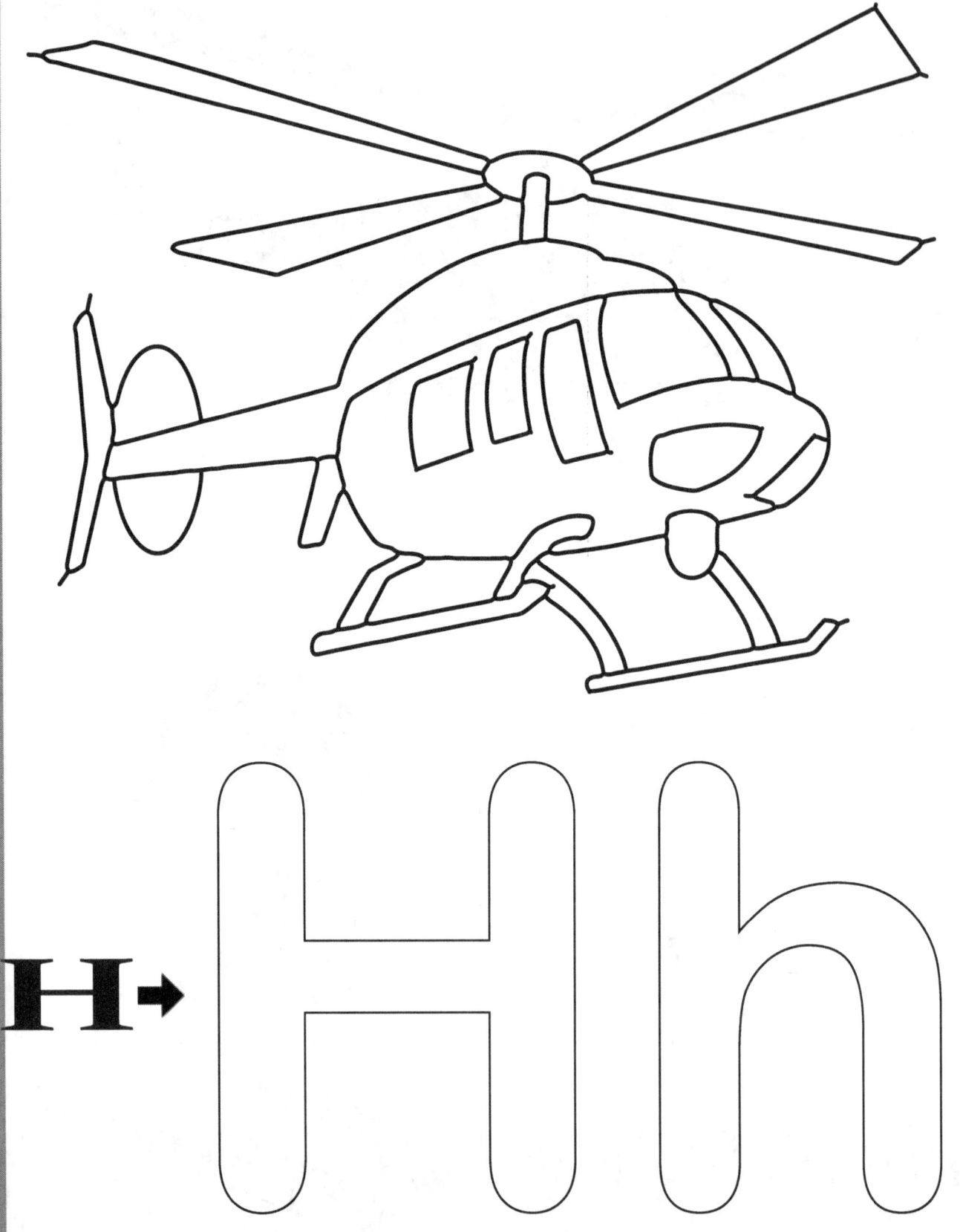

H →

H

h

H

h

H

h

H

h

I for Iron

I ➤ Insect	
I ➤ Igloo	
I ➤ Ice cream	

let,s to color

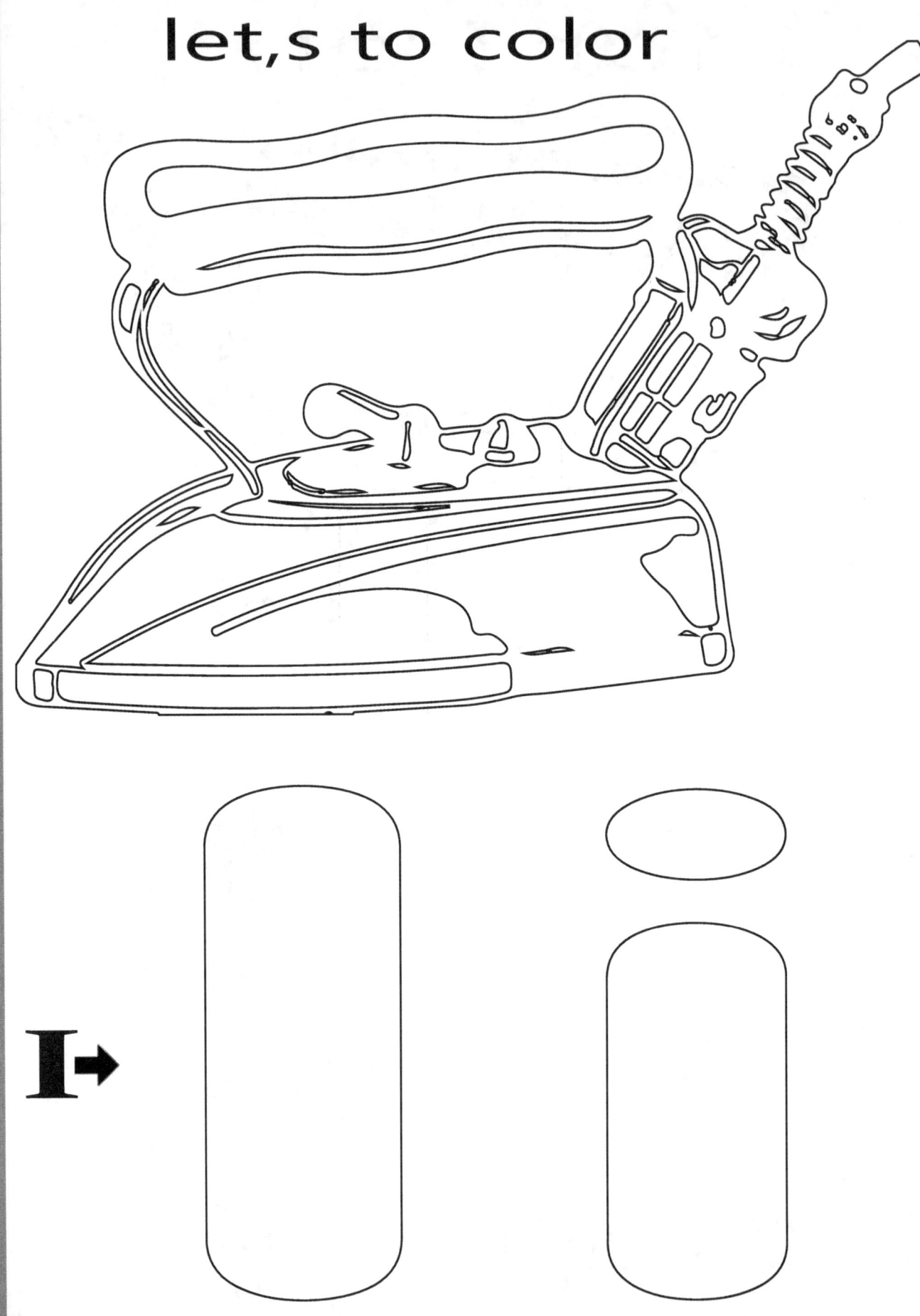

I

i

I

i

I

i

I

i

J for jackal

J➡Jug	
J➡Jump	
J➡Jeep	

let,s to color

J➡

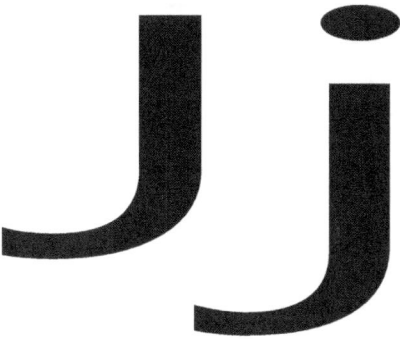

J j

J J J J J

j j j j j

J J J J J

j j j j j

J J J J J

j j j j j

J J J J J

j j j j j

K FOR KANGAROO

K ➡ Keyboard	
K ➡ Key	
K ➡ Kite	

let,s to color

K➡

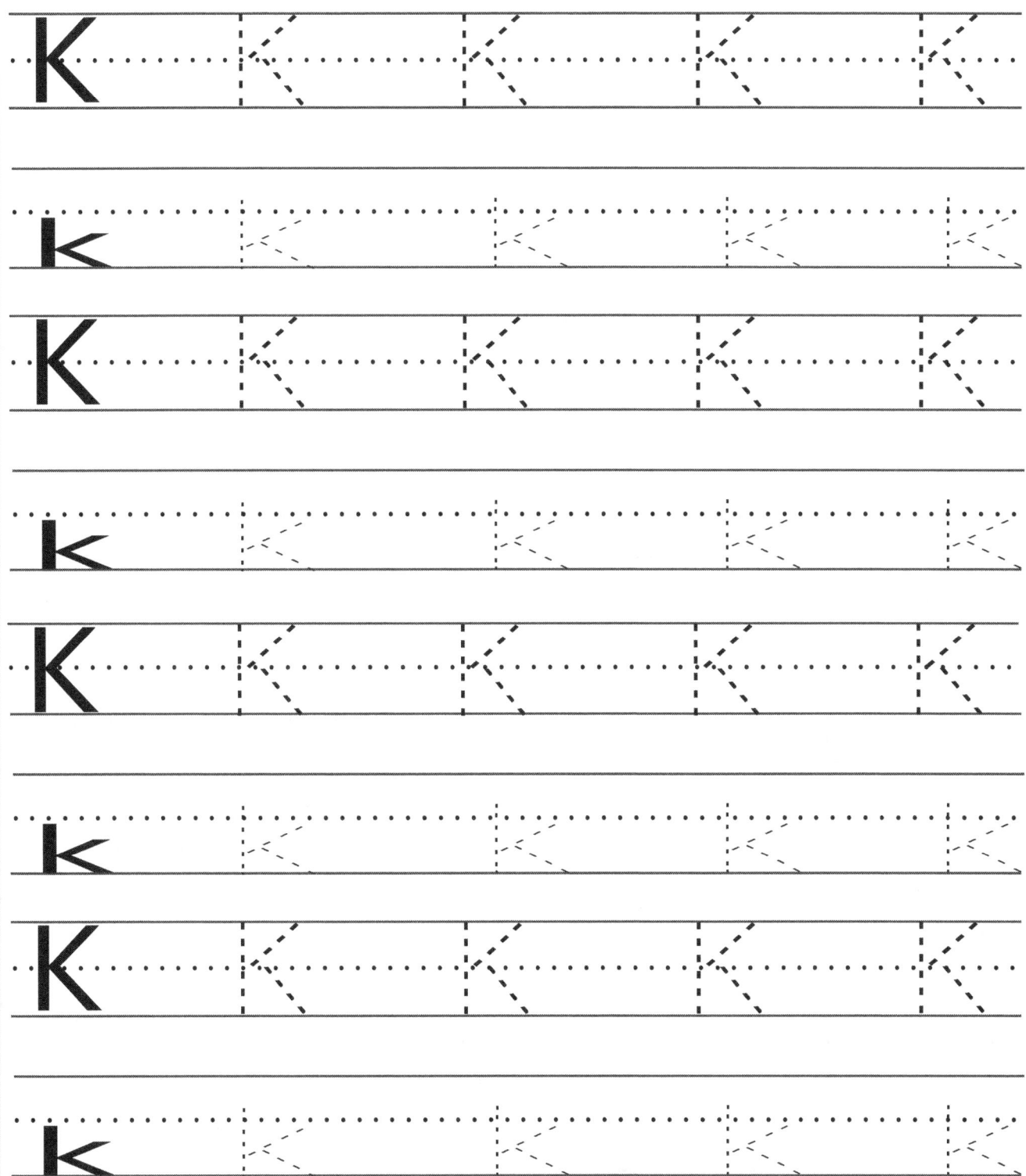

L for Leaf

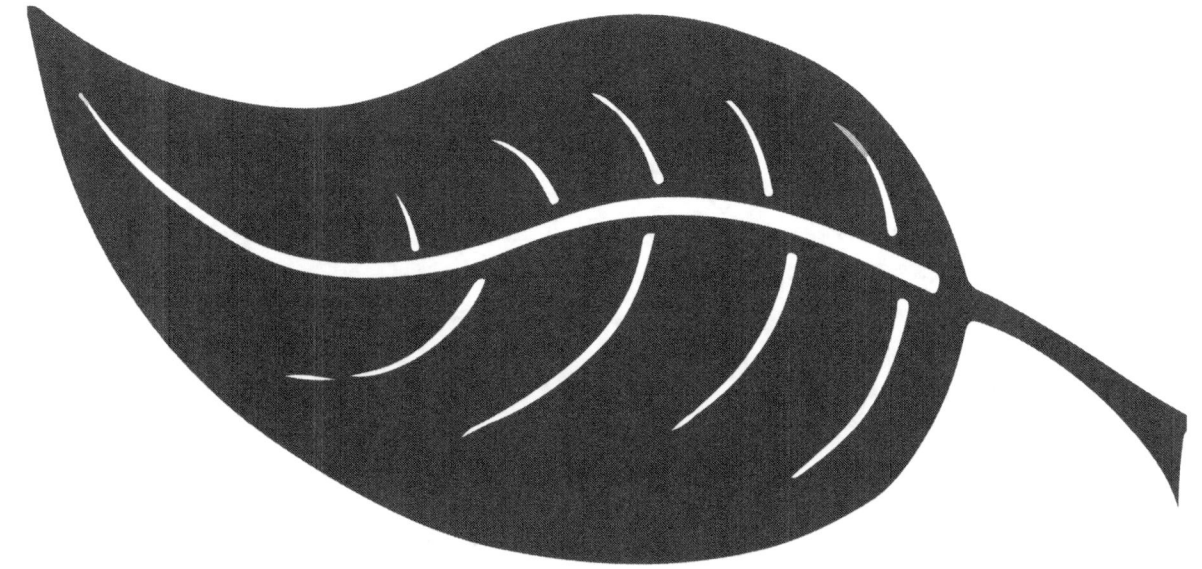

L ➔ Leg	
L ➔ Lion	
L ➔ Lip	

let,s to color

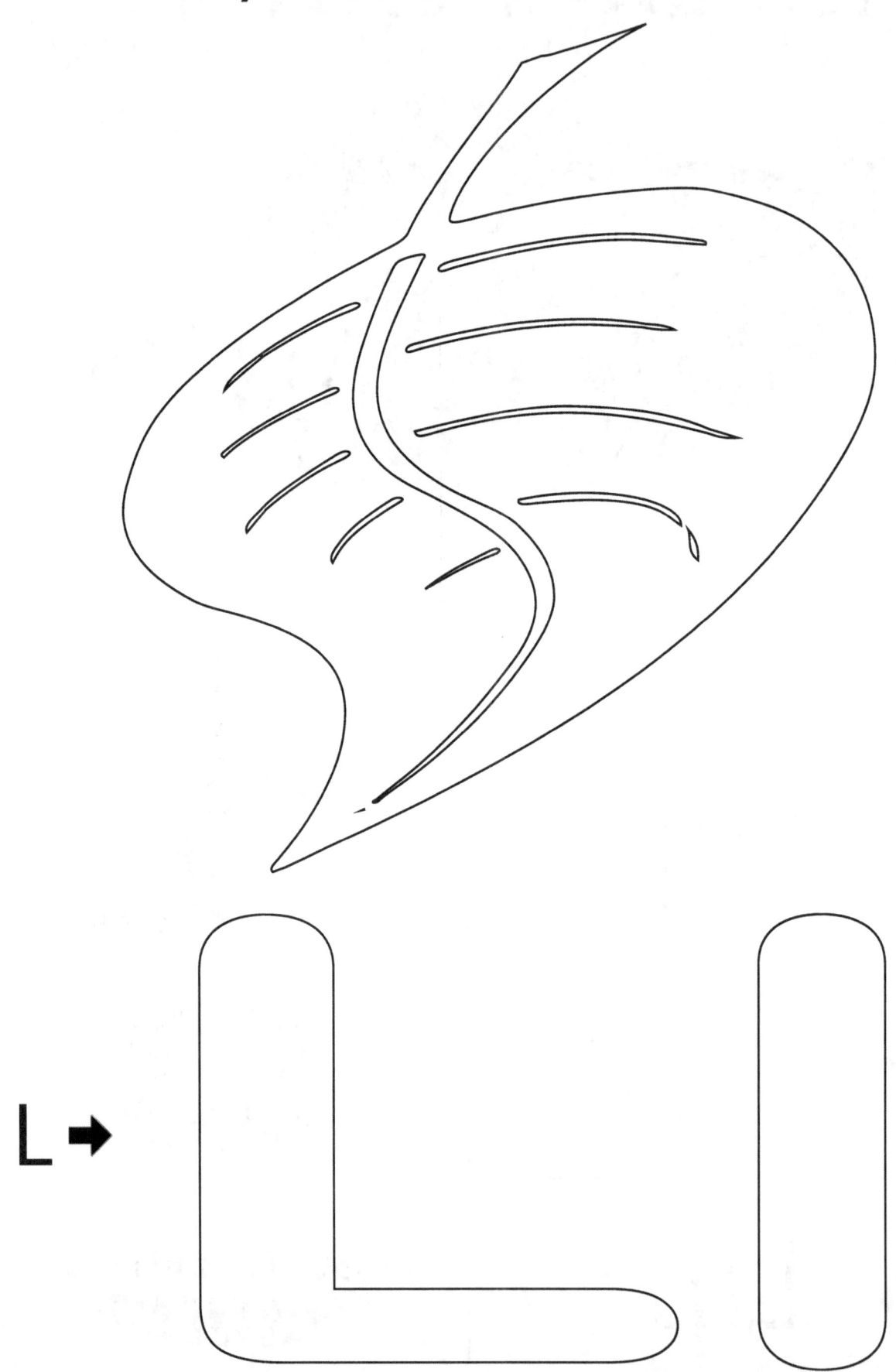

L →

L · · · L ·

I · · · I ·

L · · · L ·

I · · · I ·

L · · · L ·

I · · · I ·

L · · · L ·

I · · · I ·

M for Mug

M → Monkey	
M → Mouse	
M → Mosquito	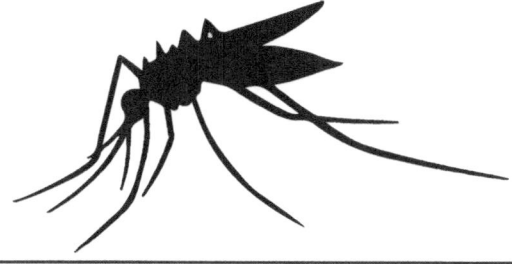

let,s to color

M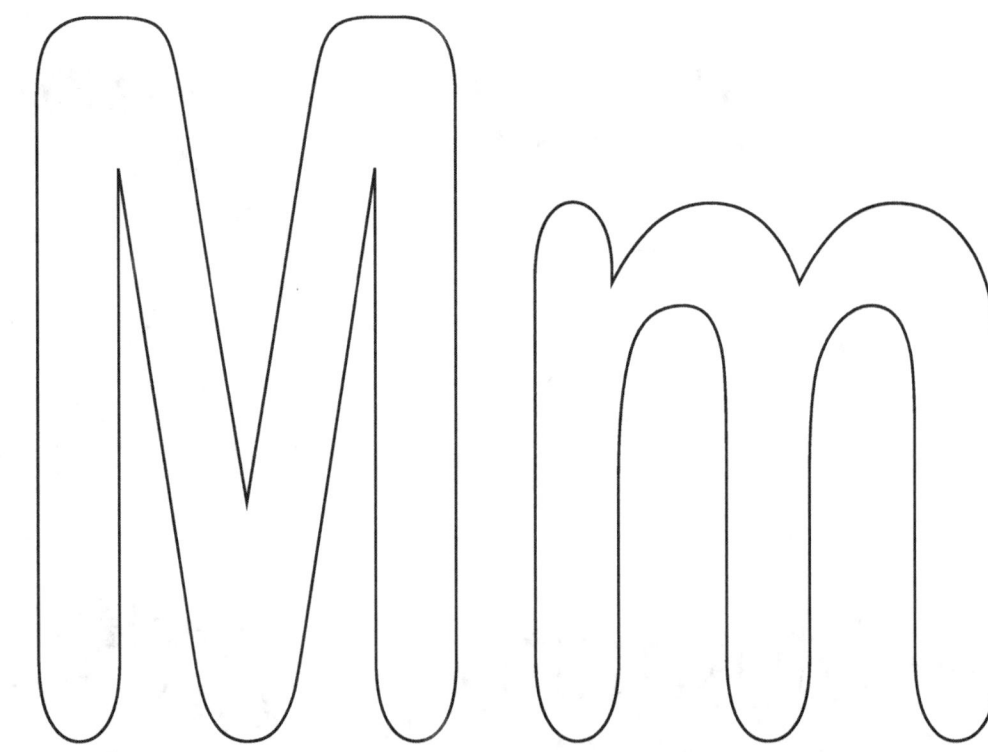

M m

M M M M M M M M M M

m m m m m m m m m m

M M M M M M M M M M

m m m m m m m m m m

M M M M M M M M M M

m m m m m m m m m m

M M M M M M M M M M

m m m m m m m m m m

N for Nut

N ➔ **Nest**	
N ➔ **Nib**	
N ➔ **Net**	

let,s to color

N→

N n

N · · · · · N · · · N · · · N · · · N · · ·

n · · · · n · · n · · n · · n · ·

N · · · · · N · · · N · · · N · · · N · · ·

n · · · · n · · n · · n · · n · ·

N · · · · · N · · · N · · · N · · · N · · ·

n · · · · n · · n · · n · · n · ·

N · · · · · N · · · N · · · N · · · N · · ·

n · · · · n · · n · · n · · n · ·

O for Owl

O → **Onion**	
O → Ox	
O → Orca	

let,s to color

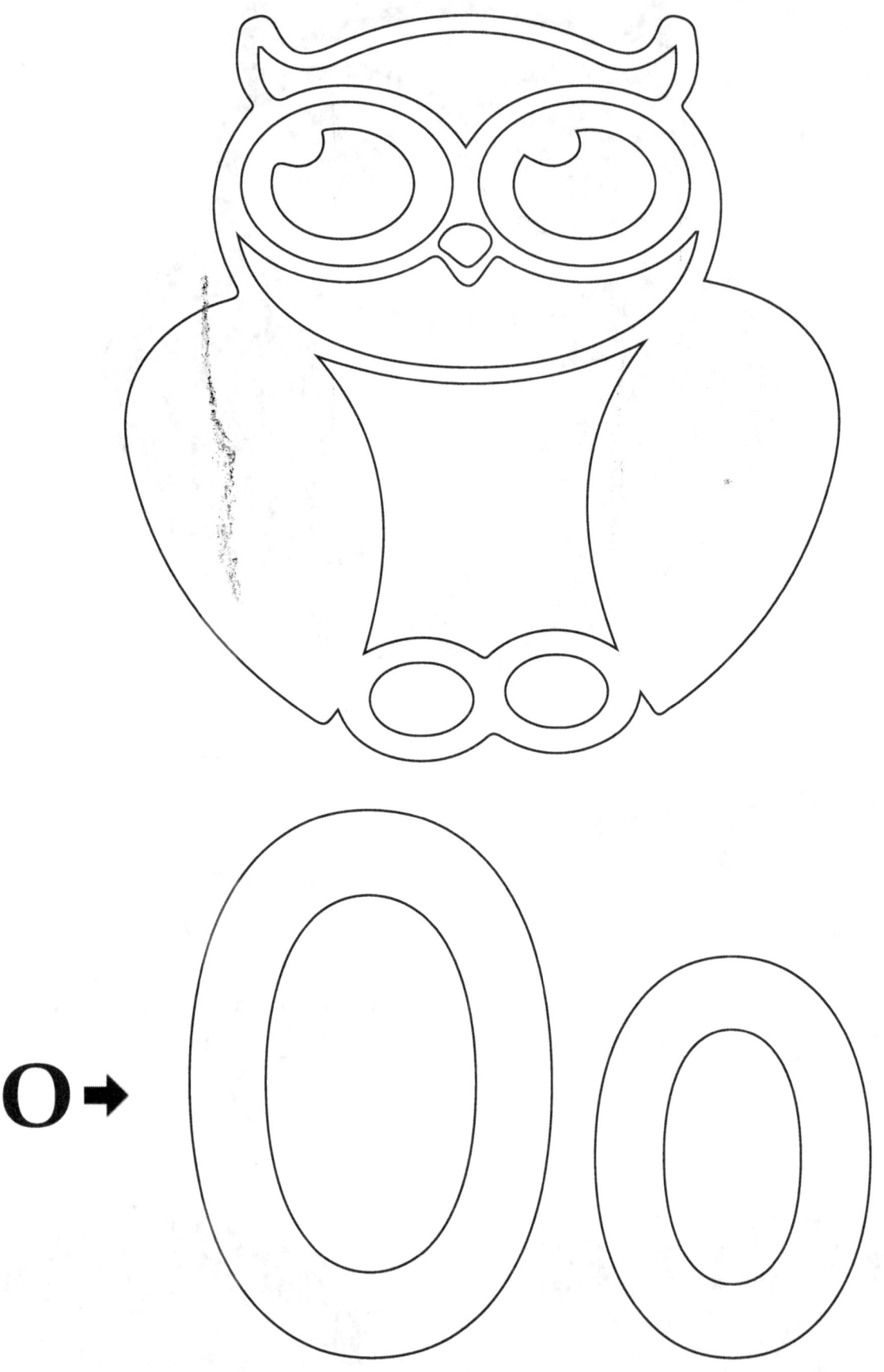

O→

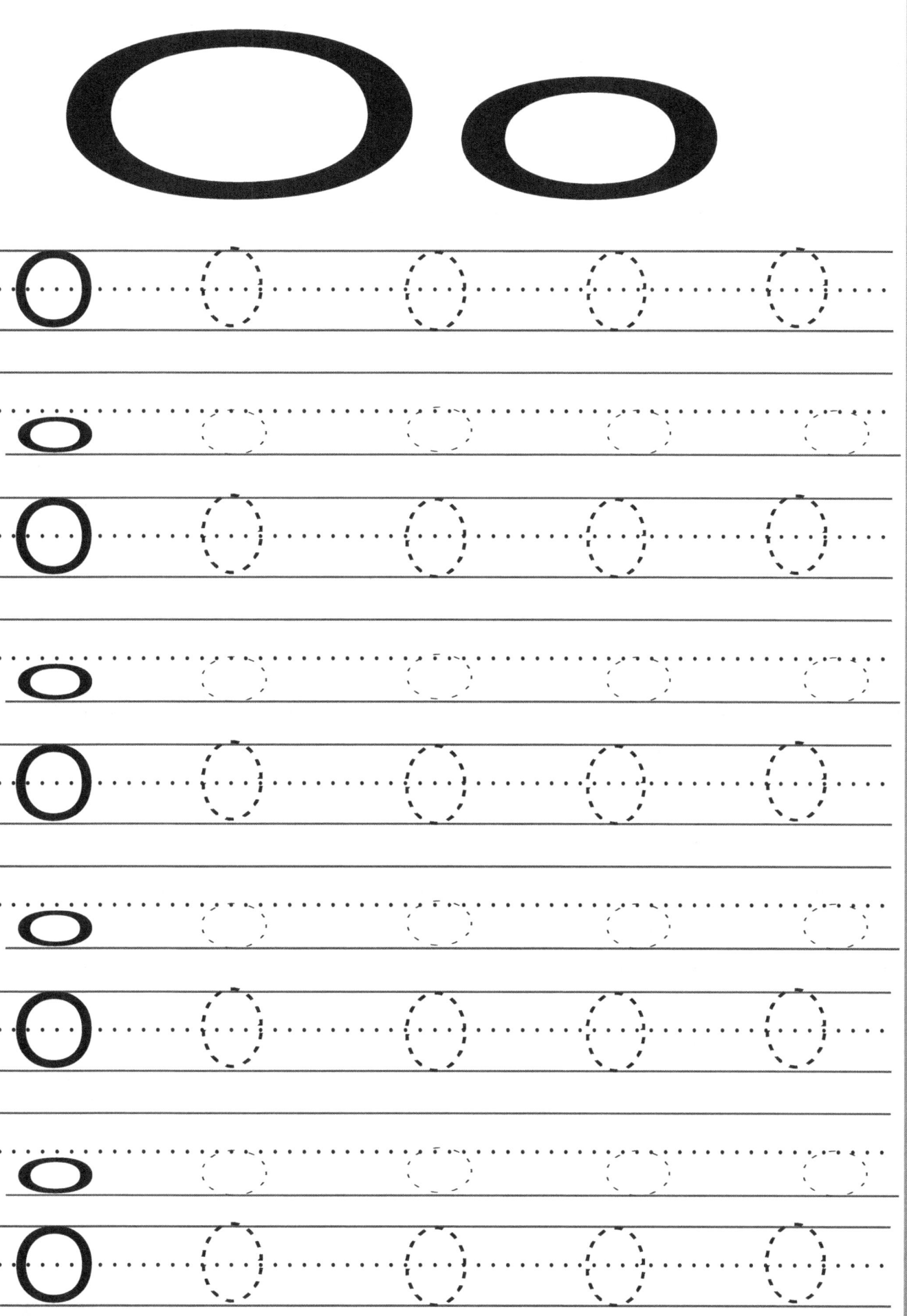

P for piano

P ➤ Pig	
P ➤ Pigeon	
P ➤ Planet	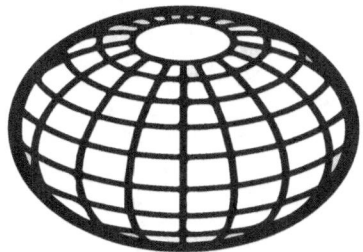

let,s to color

P ➡

Pp

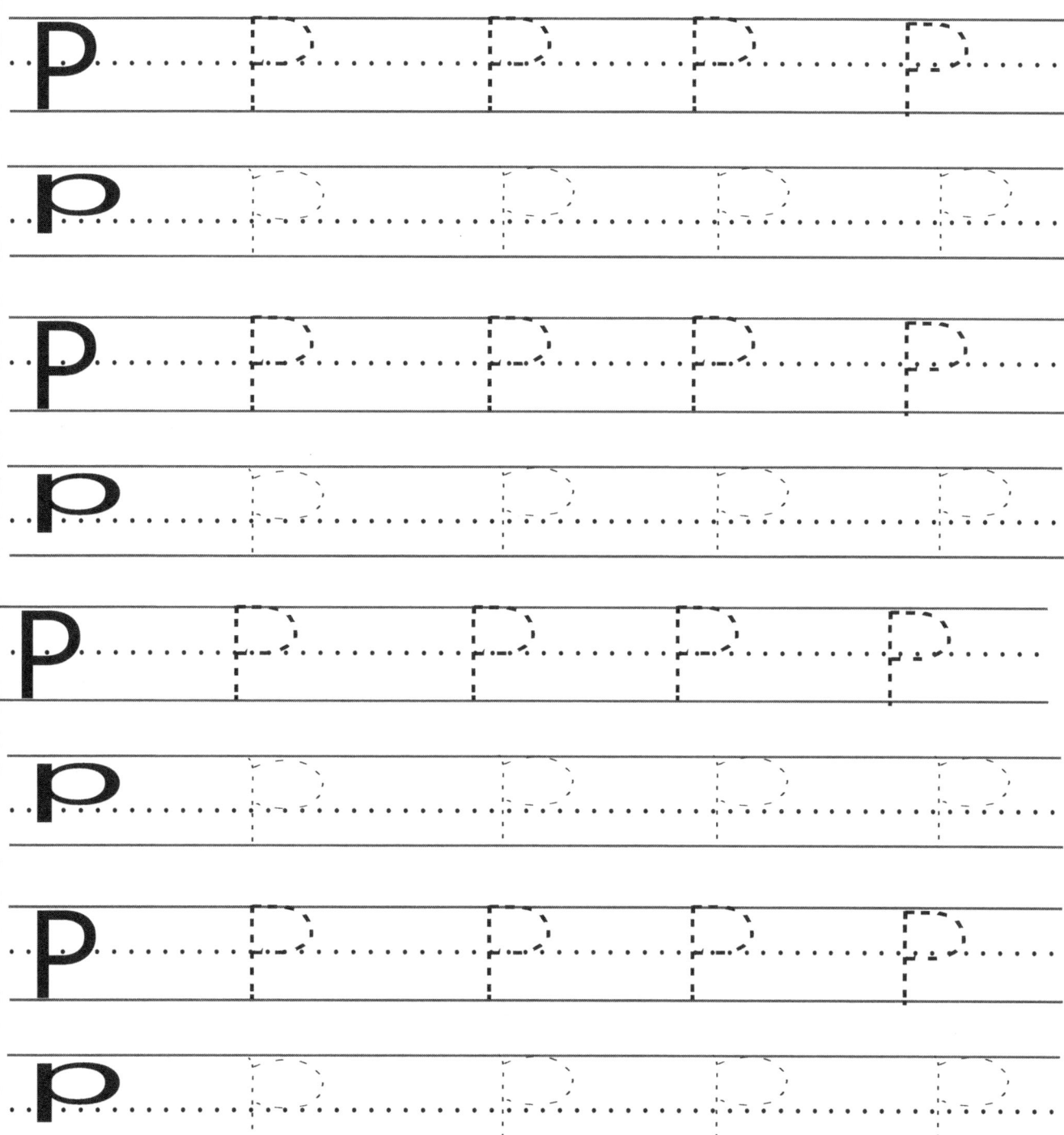

Q for Quads

Q → Quial	
Q → Queen	
Q → Quoll	

let,s to color

Q→

Q q

Q Q Q Q Q

q q q q q

Q Q Q Q Q

q q q q q

Q Q Q Q Q

q q q q q

Q Q Q Q Q

q q q q q

q q q q q

R for Remote

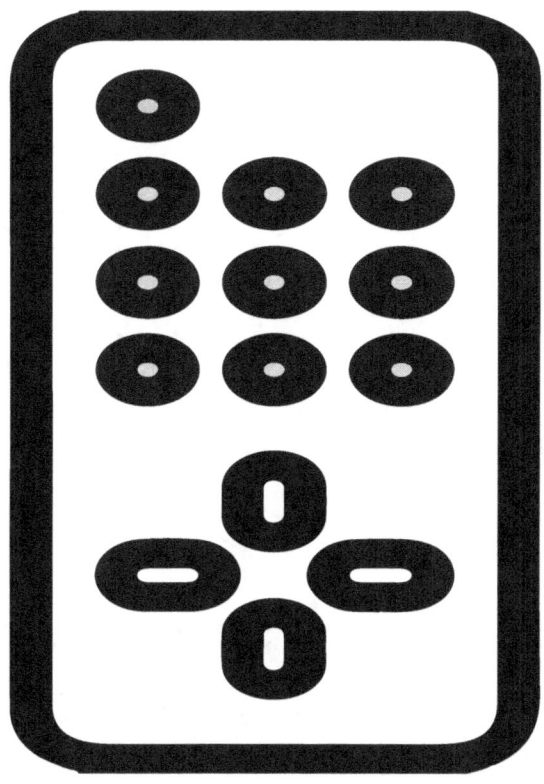

R ➜ Rat	
R ➜ Roof	
R ➜ Rock	

let,s to color

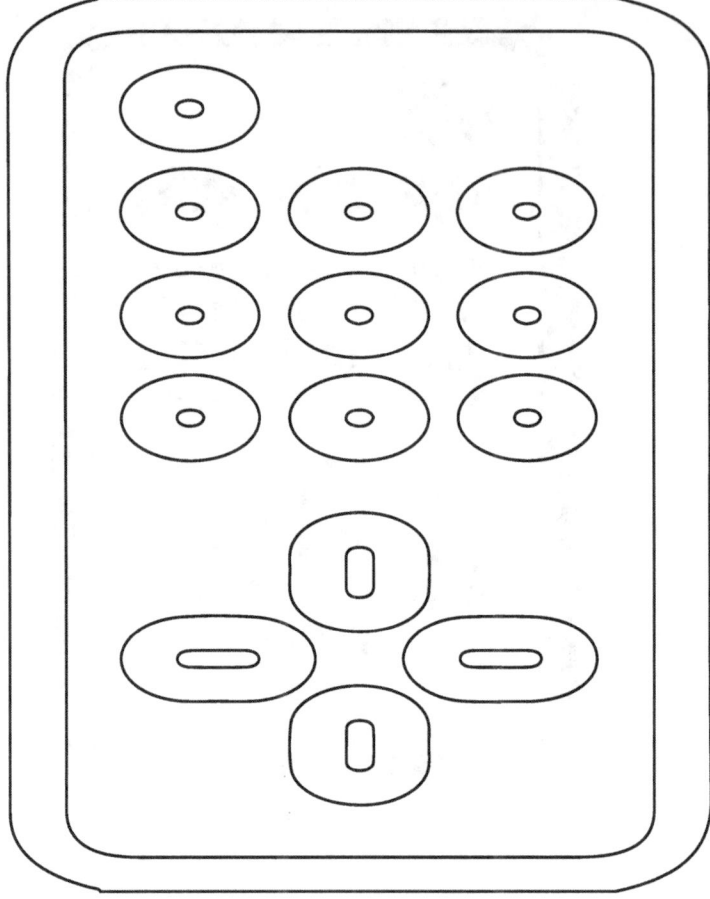

R➜

Rr

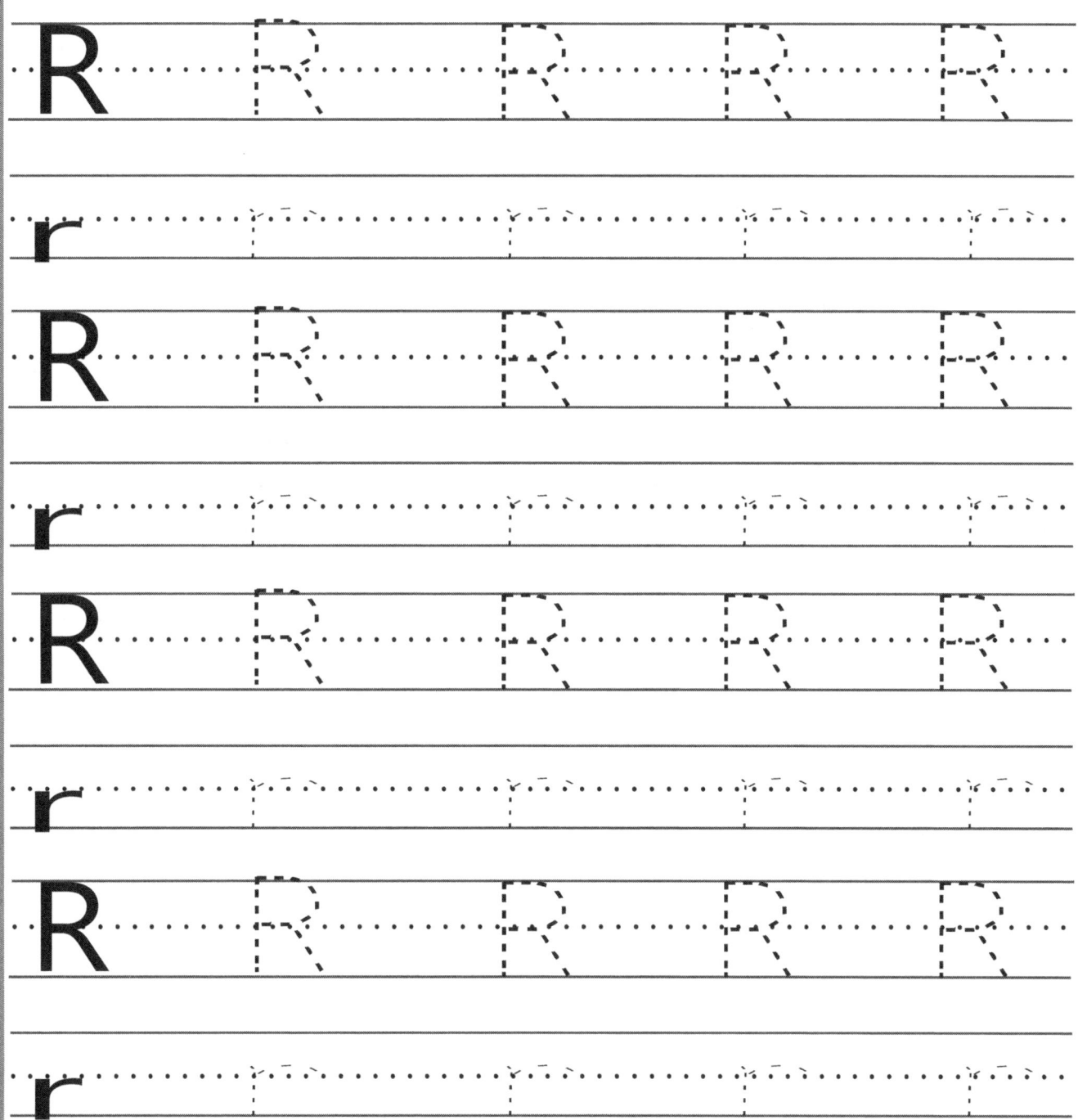

S for Shoes

S→ Star	
S→ Sun	
S→ Shark	

let,s to color

S→

S s

S   S   S   S   S

s   s   s   s

S   S   S   S   S

s   s   s   s

S   S   S   S   S

s   s   s   s

S   S   S   S

s   s   s   s

T for tree

T → Tiger	
T → Tractor	
T → Tomato	

let,s to color

T ➡

T t

T
t
T
t
T
t
T
t

U for Umbrella

U → USB	
U → UFO	
U → Unicorn	

let,s to color

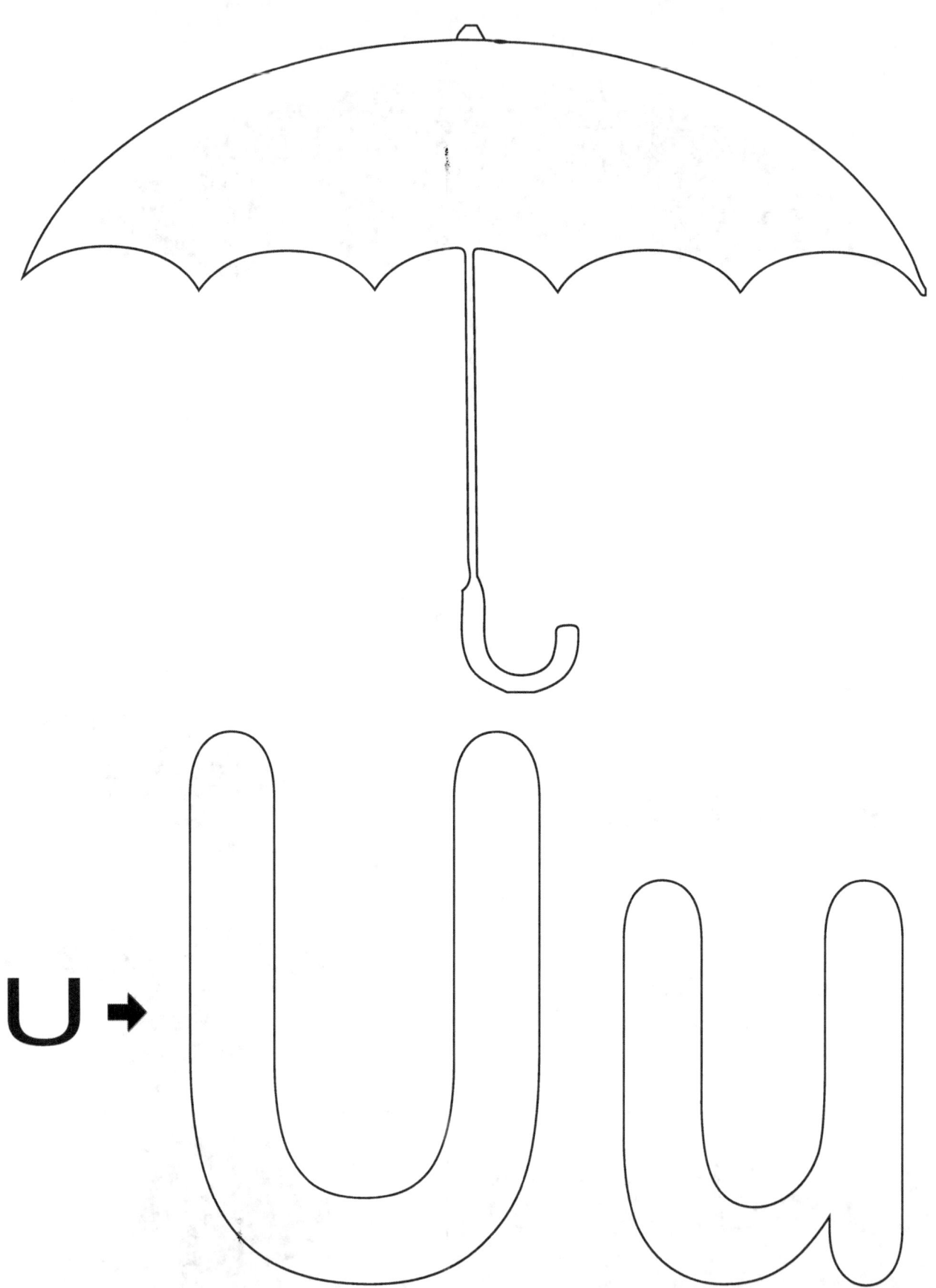

U ➤

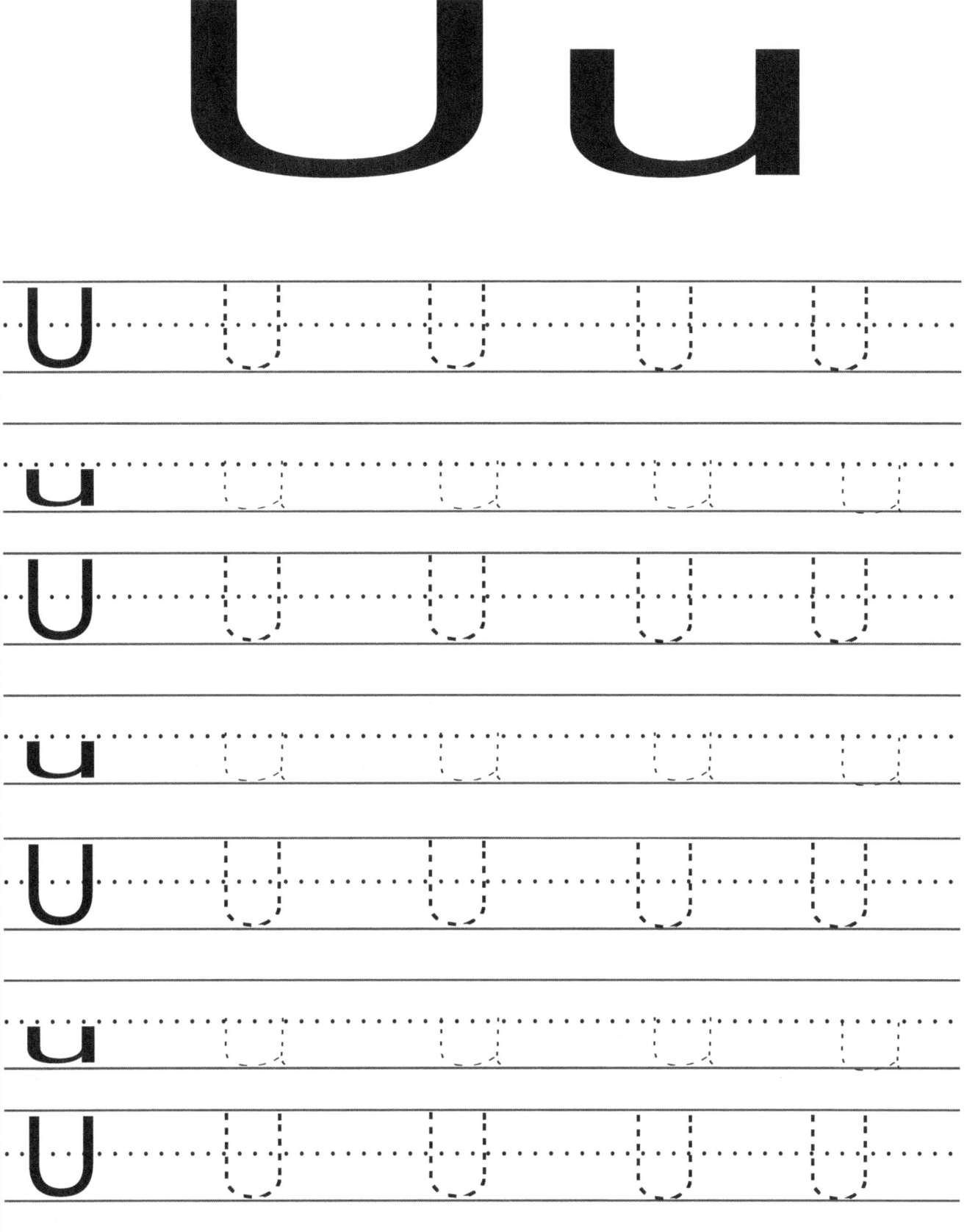

V for Vulture

V → Van	
V → Vegetable	
V → viola	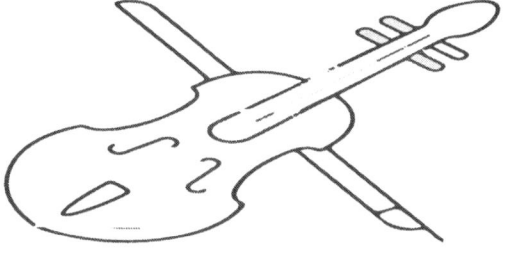

let,s to color

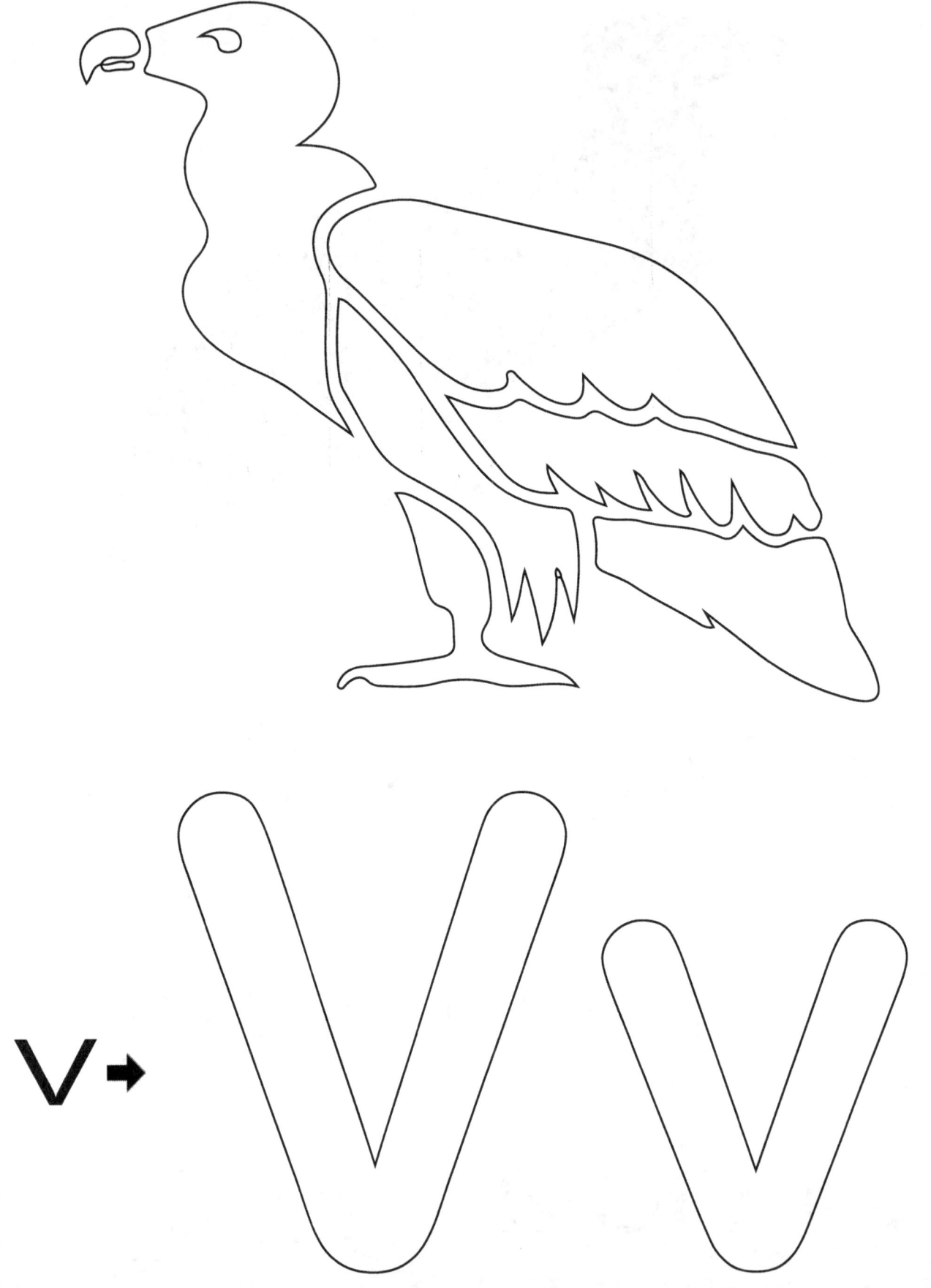

V➔

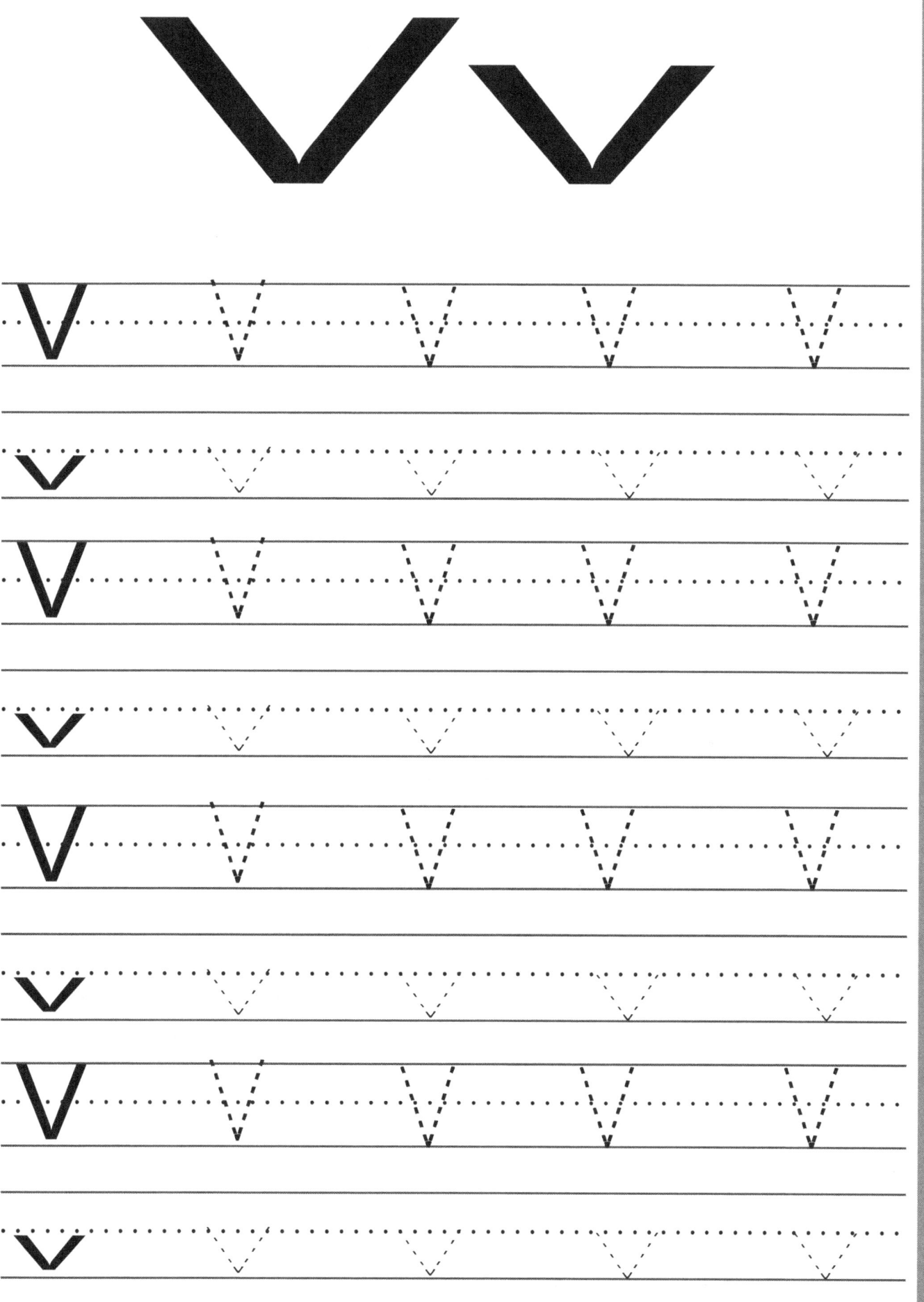

W for Window

W → Whale	
W → Wagon	
W → Wolf	

let,s to color

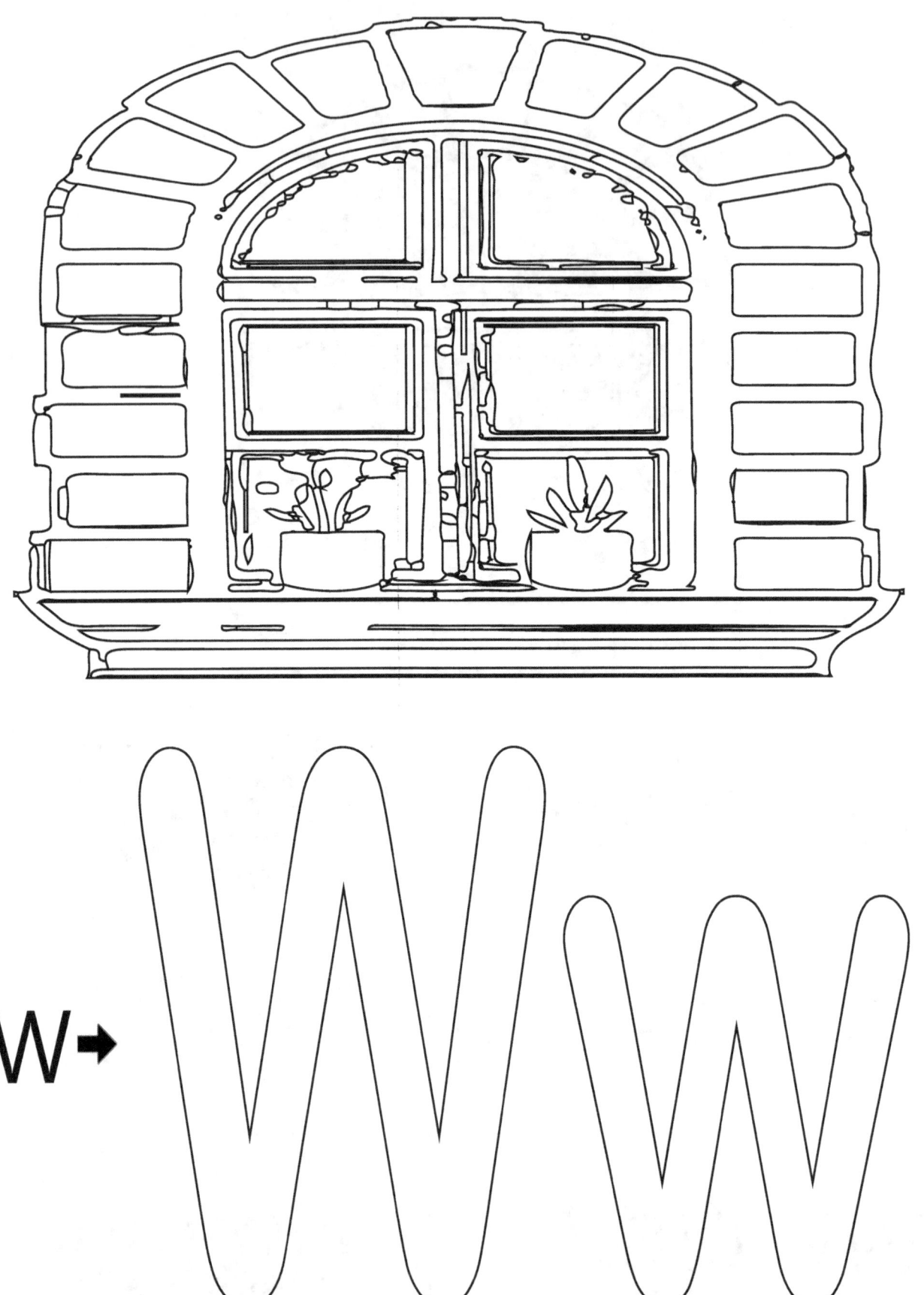

W➡

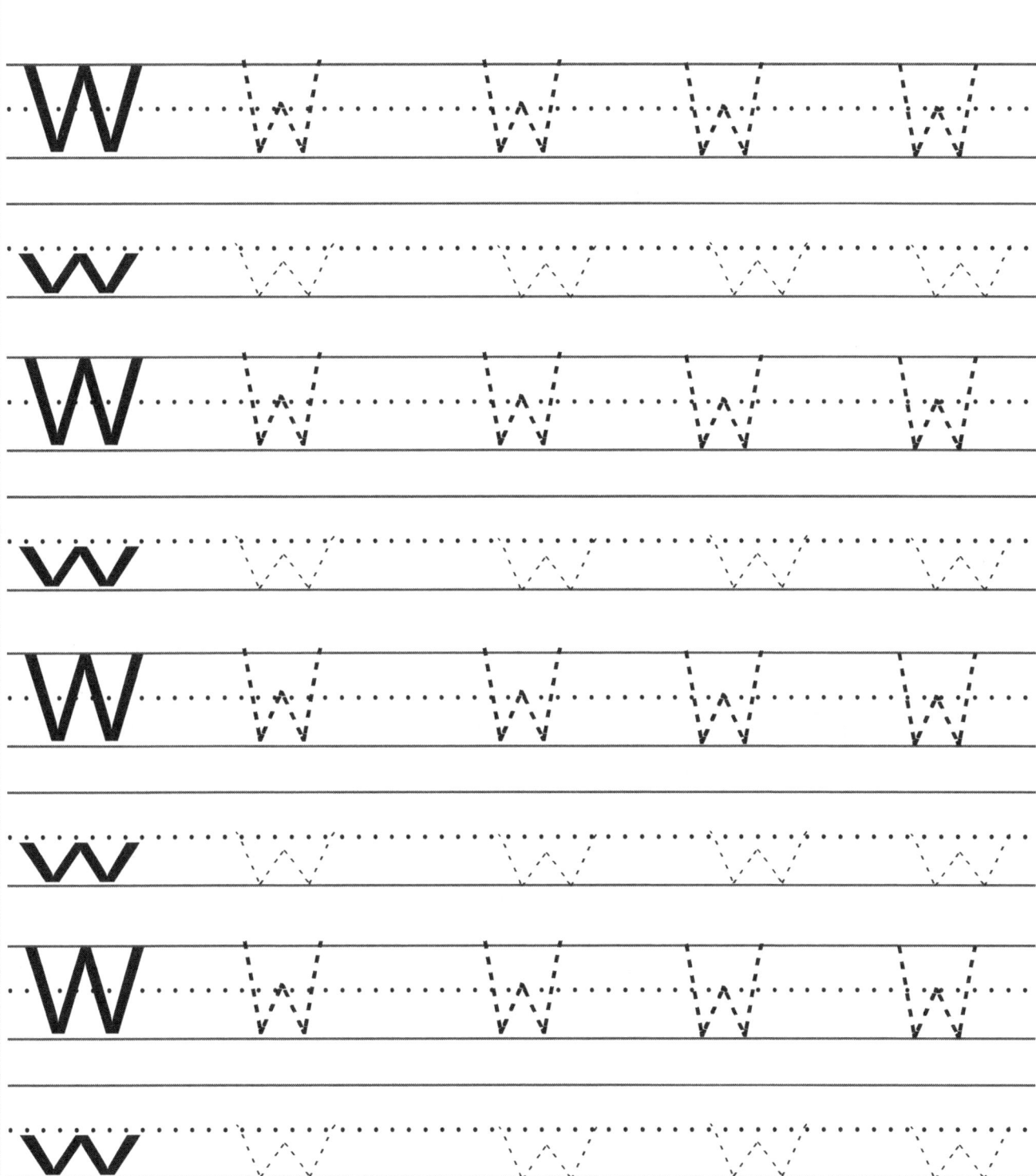

X for Xerus

x	Xylophone	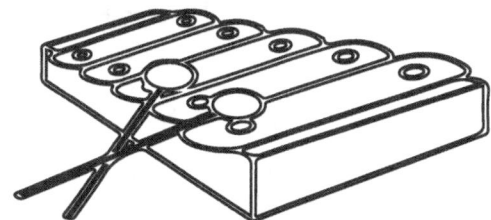
x	Xmas tree	
x	X ray Fish	

let,s to color

X

X· · · · · · · · · X· · · · · · · · · X· · · · · · · · · X· · · · · · · · · X

X· · · · · · · · · X· · · · · · · · · X· · · · · · · · · X· · · · · · · · · X

X· · · · · · · · · X· · · · · · · · · X· · · · · · · · · X· · · · · · · · · X

X· · · · · · · · · X· · · · · · · · · X· · · · · · · · · X· · · · · · · · · X

X· · · · · · · · · X· · · · · · · · · X· · · · · · · · · X· · · · · · · · · X

X· · · · · · · · · X· · · · · · · · · X· · · · · · · · · X· · · · · · · · · X

X· · · · · · · · · X· · · · · · · · · X· · · · · · · · · X· · · · · · · · · X

X· · · · · · · · · X· · · · · · · · · X· · · · · · · · · X· · · · · · · · · X

Y for Yak

Y	yo yo	
Y	Yam	
Y	Yarn	

let,s to color

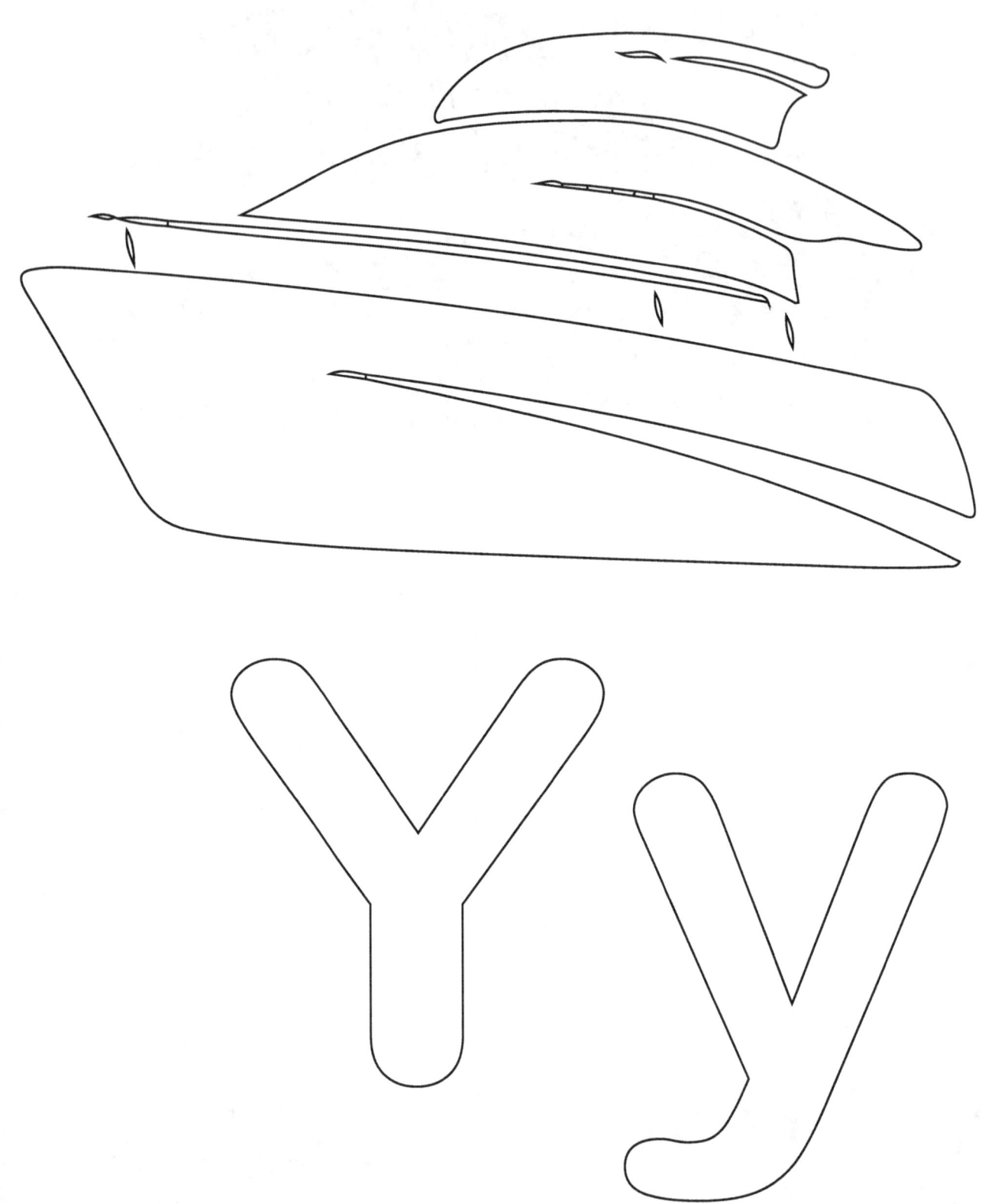

X for Xerus

X ➡ Xylophone	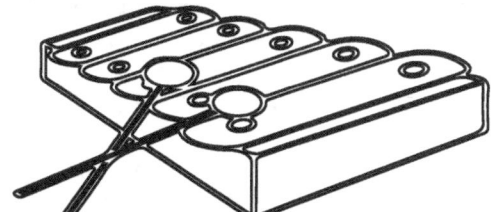
X ➡ Xmas tree	
X ➡ X ray Fish	

To Color

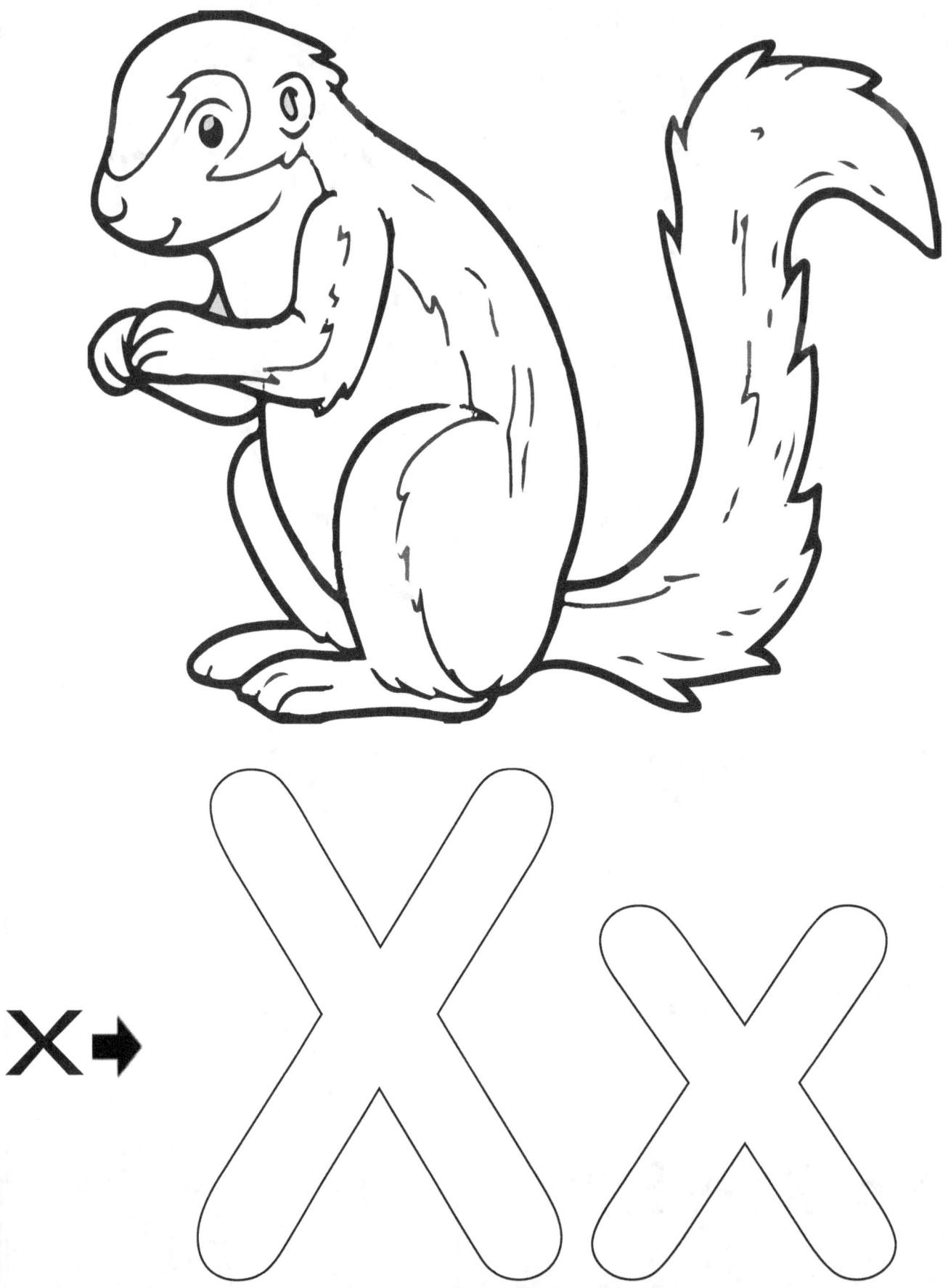

X➡ X X

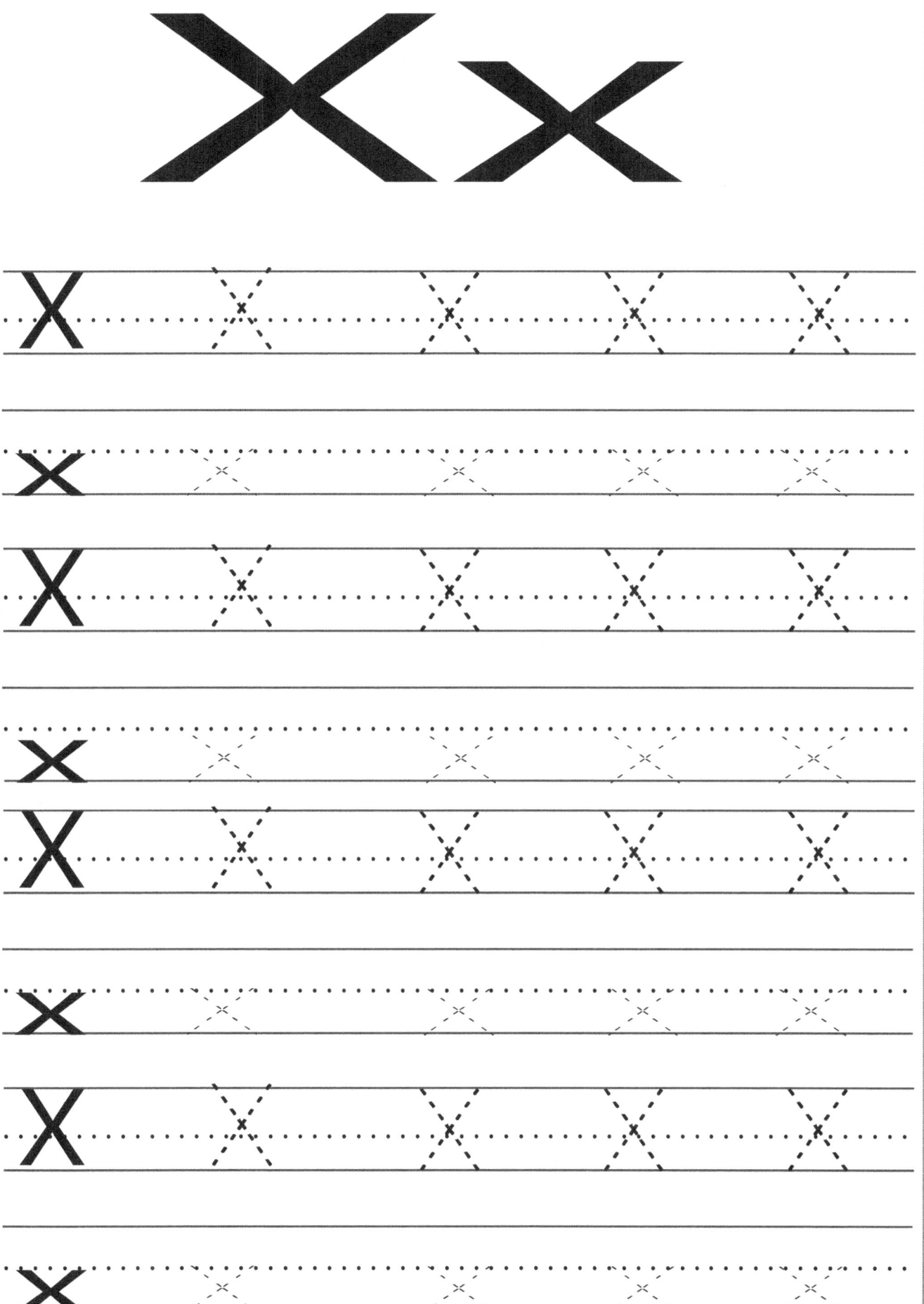

Y for Yak

Y ➡ yo yo	
Y ➡ Yam	
Y ➡ Yarn	

let,s to color

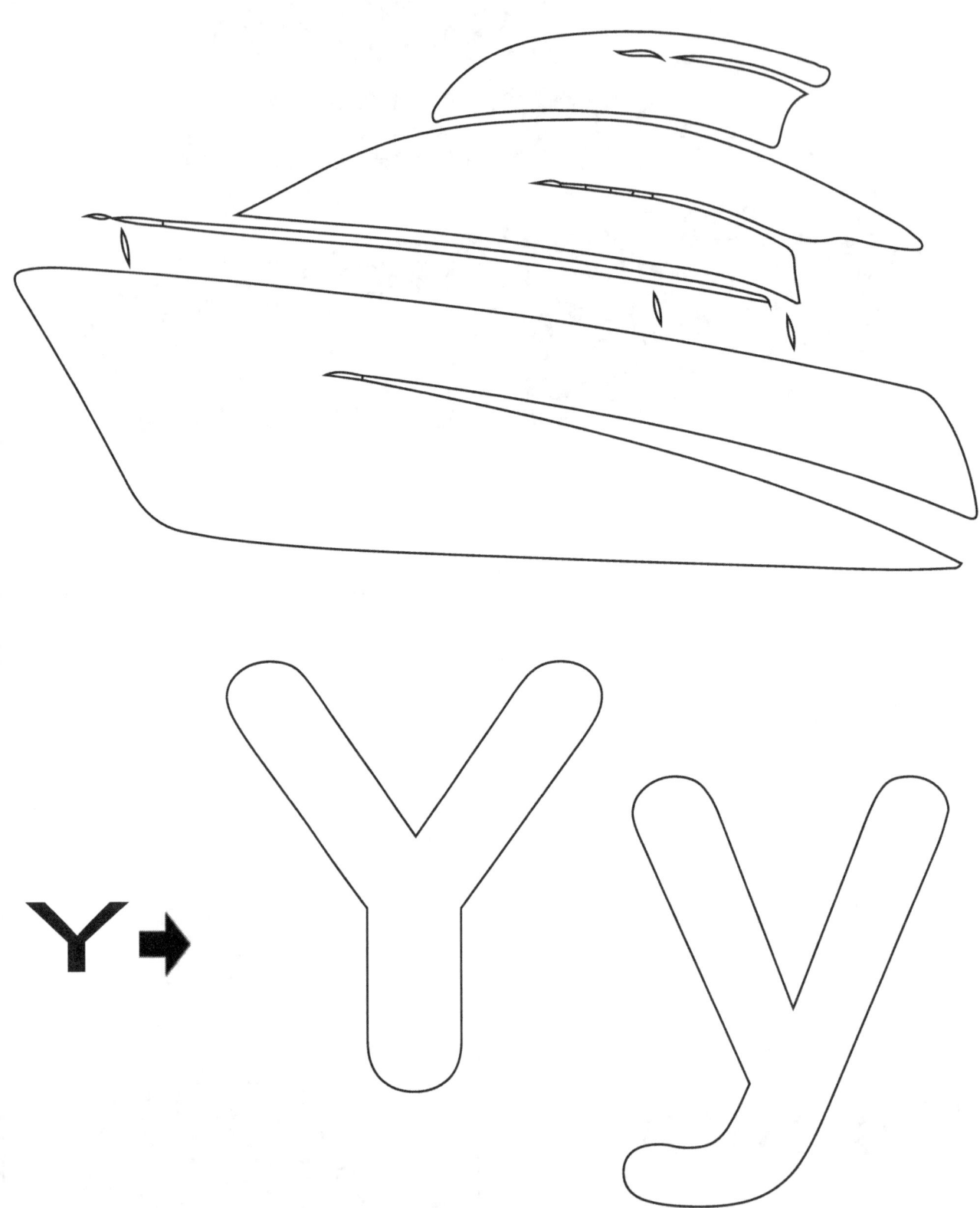

Y ➡

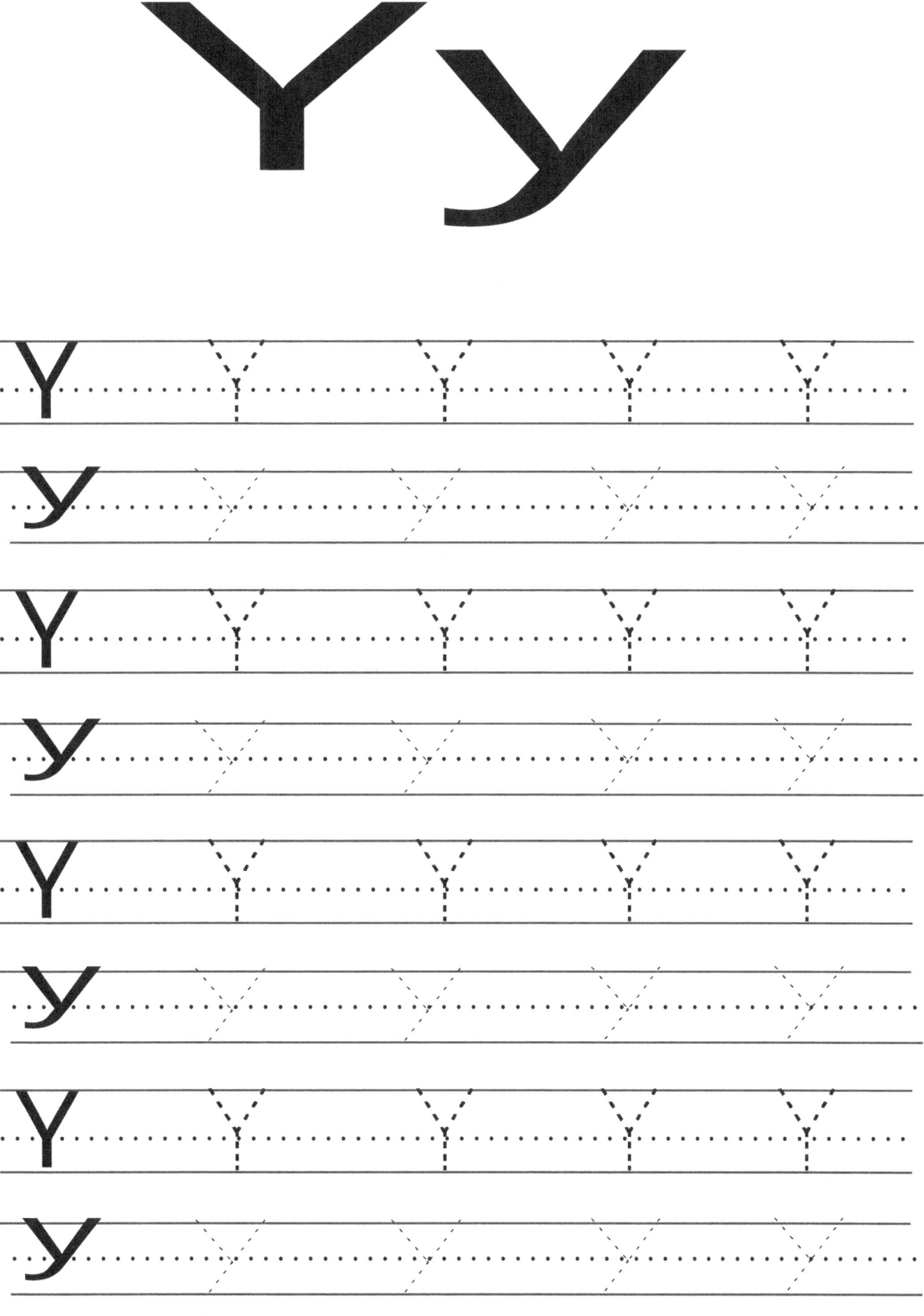

Z for Zebra

Z ➡ Zip	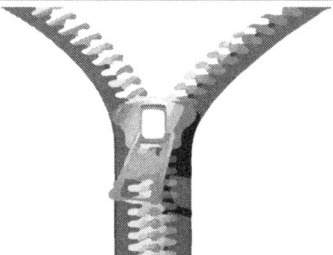
Z ➡ Zoo	
Z ➡ Zeus	

let,s to color

z ➡

Zz

Z
Z
Z
Z
Z
Z
Z
Z
Z

One **1** =

1

One   One   One   One   One

1

One   One   One   One   One

1

One   One   One   One   One

1

One   One   One   One   One

Practice To Letter

Two 2 =

2

Two Two Two Two Two

2

Two Two Two Two Two

2

Two Two Two Two Two

2

Two Two Two Two Two

Practice To Letter

Three 3 =

3

3 .... 3 .... 3 .... 3 ..... 3 3

Three   Three   Three   Three

3 .... 3 .... 3 .... 3 ..... 3 3

Three   Three   Three   Three

3 .... 3 .... 3 .... 3 ..... 3 3

Three   Three   Three   Three

3 .... 3 .... 3 .... 3 ..... 3 3

Three   Three   Three   Three

Practice To Letter

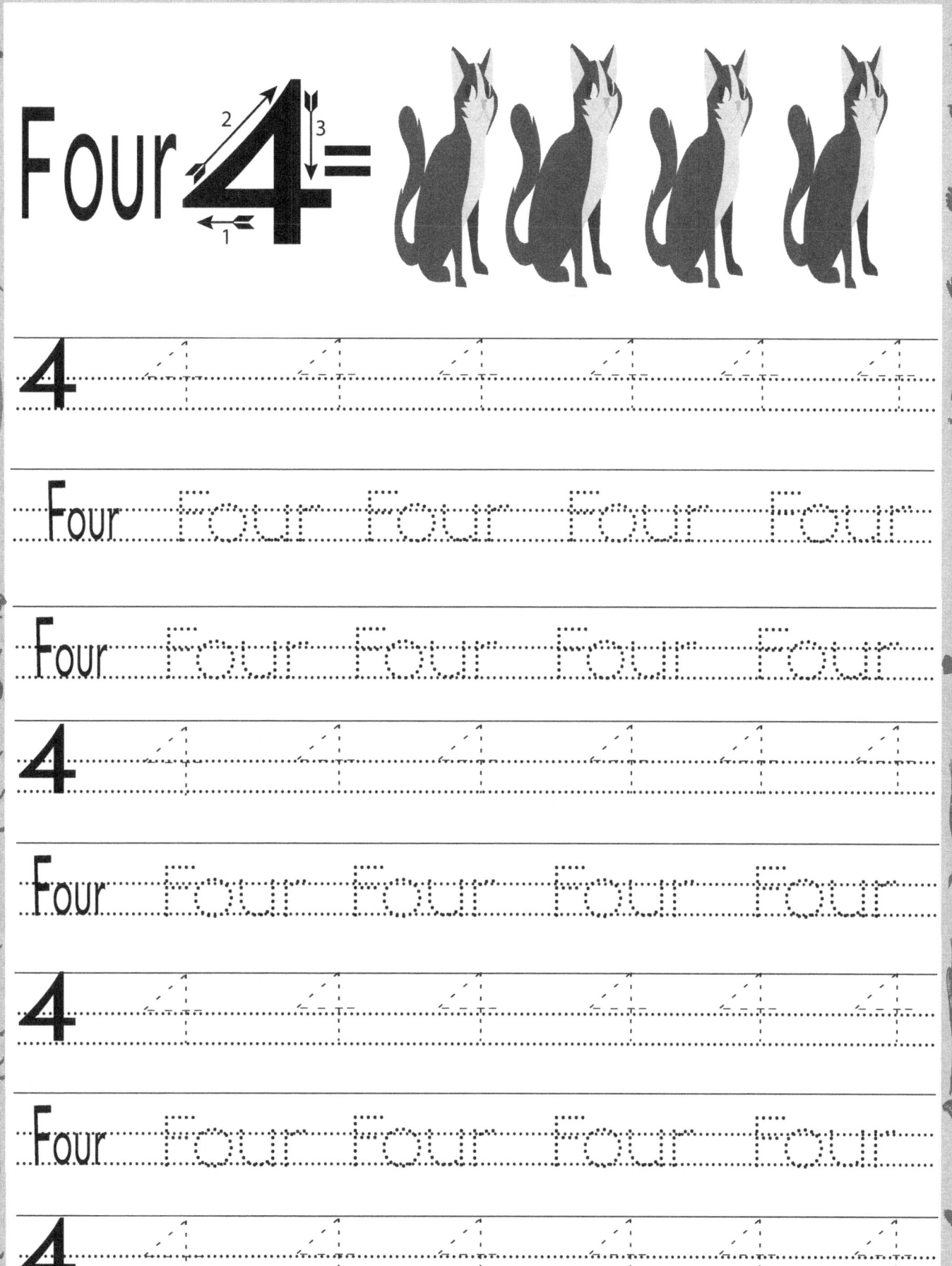

Four 4 =

4   4   4   4   4   4

Four   Four   Four   Four   Four

Four   Four   Four   Four   Four

4   4   4   4   4   4

Four   Four   Four   Four   Four

4   4   4   4   4   4

Four   Four   Four   Four   Four

4   4   4   4   4   4

Practice To Letter

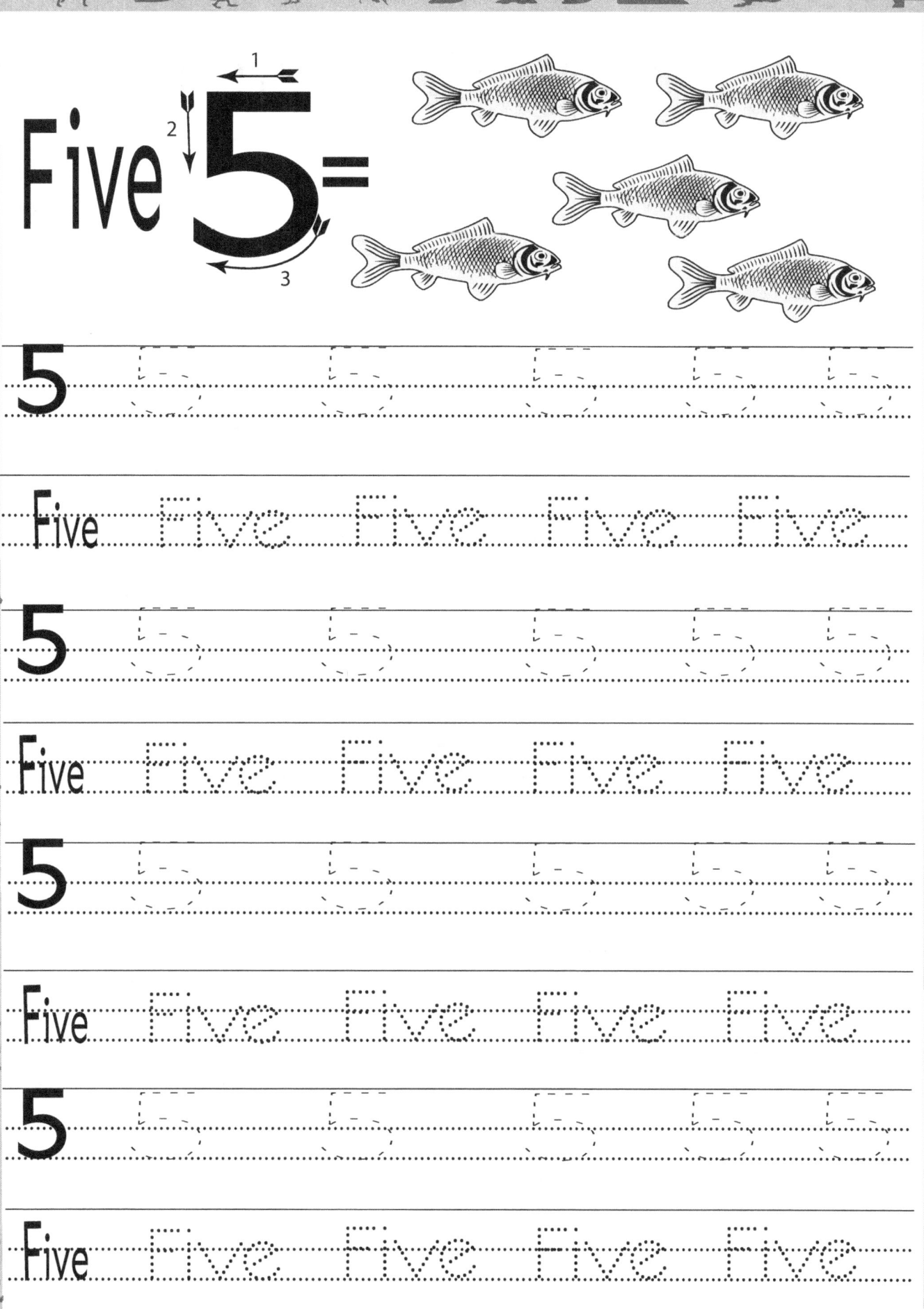

Five ^{2}5$=$

5 5 5 5 5 5

Five Five Five Five Five

5 5 5 5 5 5

Five Five Five Five Five

5 5 5 5 5 5

Five Five Five Five Five

5 5 5 5 5 5

Five Five Five Five Five

Practice To Letter

Six 6 =
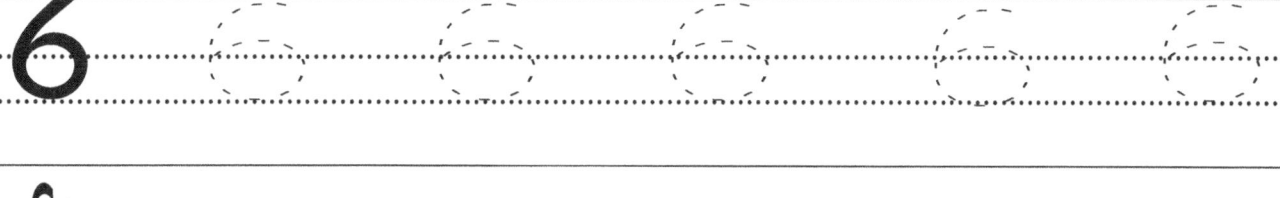

6

Six   Six   Six   Six   Six   Six

6

Six   Six   Six   Six   Six   Six

6

Six   Six   Six   Six   Six   Six

6

Six   Six   Six   Six   Six   Six

Practice To Letter

Seven 7 =

7
....

Seven ... Seven ... Seven ... Seven ... Seven

7
....

Seven ... Seven ... Seven ... Seven ... Seven

7
....

Seven ... Seven ... Seven ... Seven ... Seven

7
....

Seven ... Seven ... Seven ... Seven ... Seven

Practice To Letter

Eight 8 =

8   8   8   8   8   8

Eight   Eight   Eight   Eight   Eight

8   8   8   8   8   8

Eight   Eight   Eight   Eight   Eight

8   8   8   8   8   8

Eight   Eight   Eight   Eight   Eight

8   8   8   8   8   8

Eight   Eight   Eight   Eight   Eight

Practice To Letter

Nine 9 =

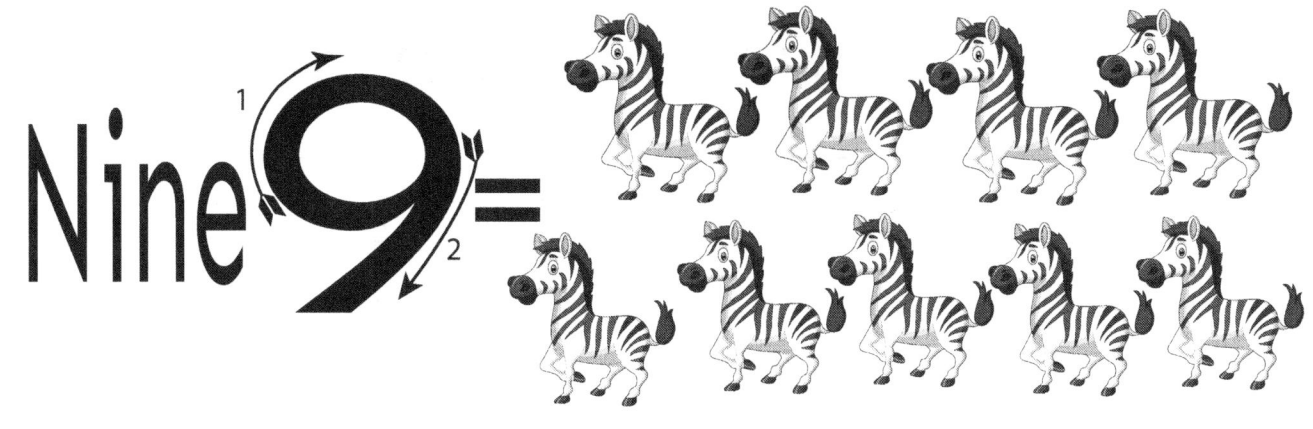

9   9   9   9   9   9

Nine   Nine   Nine   Nine   Nine

9   9   9   9   9   9

Nine   Nine   Nine   Nine   Nine

9   9   9   9   9   9

Nine   Nine   Nine   Nine   Nine

9   9   9   9   9   9

Nine   Nine   Nine   Nine   Nine

Practice To Letter

Ten 10 =

10   10   10   10   10   10

Ten   Ten   Ten   Ten   Ten   Ten

10   10   10   10   10   10

Ten   Ten   Ten   Ten   Ten   Ten

10   10   10   10   10   10

Ten   Ten   Ten   Ten   Ten   Ten

10   10   10   10   10   10

Ten   Ten   Ten   Ten   Ten   Ten

Practice To Letter

Practice writing the following words.

Lowercase

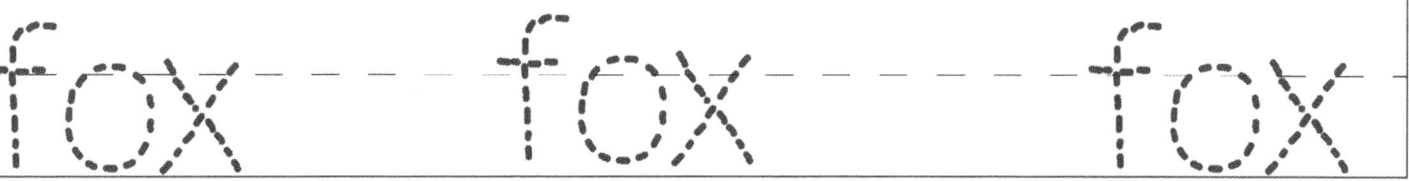

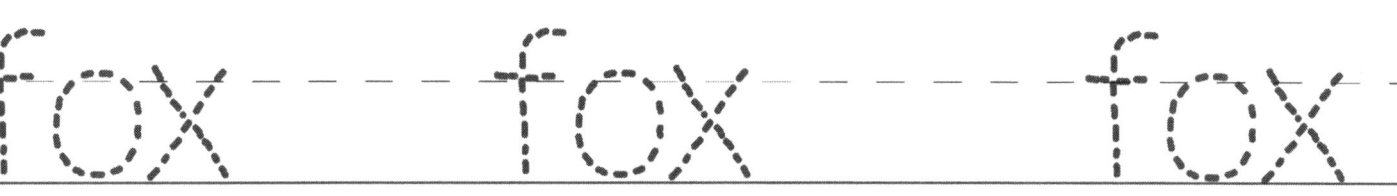

Uppercase

Trace and Color the following Animal

Practice To Letter

Practice writing the following words.

Lowercase

panda   panda

panda   panda

Uppercase

PANDA   PANDA

Trace and Color the following Animal

Practice To Letter

Practice writing the following words.

Lowercase

bear   bear   bear

bear   bear   bear

Uppercase

BEAR BEAR BEAR

Trace and Color the following Animal

Practice To Letter

I, am, at, a

I ran

I ran

I, am, at, a

I am sad

I am sad

Practice To Letter

I, am, at, a

I am a cat

I am a cat

I, am, at, a

I am six

I am six

Practice To Letter

I, am, at, a

I am a fat cat

I am a fat cat

I, am, at, a

I am six

I am six

Practice To Letter

I, am, at, a

I am at home

I am at home

I, am, at, a

A cat at a mat

A cat at a mat

Practice To Letter

I, am, at, a

I am a fox

I am a fox

I, am, at, a

I am a fox

I am a fox

Practice To Letter

an, can, see, the

I can cut

I can cut

an, can, see, the

I can sit

I can sit

Practice To Letter

an, can, see, the

I can pat

I can pat

an, can, see, the

I can see

I can see

Practice To Letter

an, can, see, the

I can bat

I can pat

an, can, see, the

I can hop

I can hop

Practice To Letter

an, can, see, the

I see an ant

I see an ant

an, can, see, the

I can Eat

I can Eat

Practice To Letter

an, can, see, the

I can see ham

I can see ham

an, can, see, the

I can see a cap

I can see a cap

Practice To Letter

an, can, see, the

I can see a hat

I can see a hat

an, can, see, the

I can see the man

I can see the man

Practice To Letter

an, can, see, the

I can see the sun

I can see the sun

an, can, see, the

I can see the jar

I can see the jar

Practice To Letter

an, can, see, the

I can see the box

I can see the box

an, can, see, the

I can see six men

I can see six men

Practice To Letter

an, can, see, the

The dog can see

The dog can see

an, can, see, the

See the van

See the van

Practice To Letter

an, can, see, the

See the box

See the box

an, can, see, the

See the jam

See the jam

Practice To Letter

an, can, see, the

An ant can see

An ant can see

an, can, see, the

An ant can run

An ant can run

Practice To Letter

an, can, see, the

An ant can sit

An ant can sit

an, can, see, the

I can win

I can win

you, and, in, had

Can you see the map?

Can you see the map?

you, and, in, had

Can you see an ant?

Can you see an ant?

you, and, in, had

Can you see a fan?

Can you see a fan?

you, and, in, had

Can you see the cat and the bat?

Can you see the cat and the bat?

you, and, in, had

Can you see the sad cat?

Can you see the sad cat?

you, and, in, had

Can you see the red mat?

Can you see the red mat?

you, and, in, had

I can see you in
the box

I can see you in
the box

you, and, in, had

I had a map in my
van

I had a map in my
van

you, and, in, had

I had a hat and
a cap

I had a hat and
a cap

you, and, in, had

I had a cat in
a hat

I had a cat in
a hat

you, and, in, had

I had a red fan

I had a red fan

you, and, in, had

I had a map

I had a map

you, and, in, had

I had a fan

I had a fan

you, and, in, had

The man had a cat

The man had a cat

you, and, in, had

You and I had fun in the sun

You and I had fun in the sun

you, and, in, had

Mix the figs in the pot

Mix the figs in the pot

Trace The Circles

Trace The Squares

Trace The Ovals

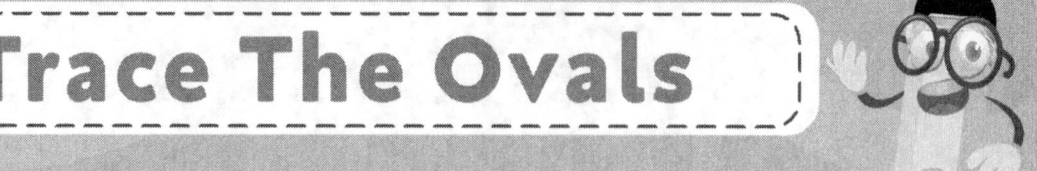

Trace The Pentagons

Trace The Rectangles

Trace The Parallelograms

Trace The Rhombuses

Trace The Stars

Trace The Hearts

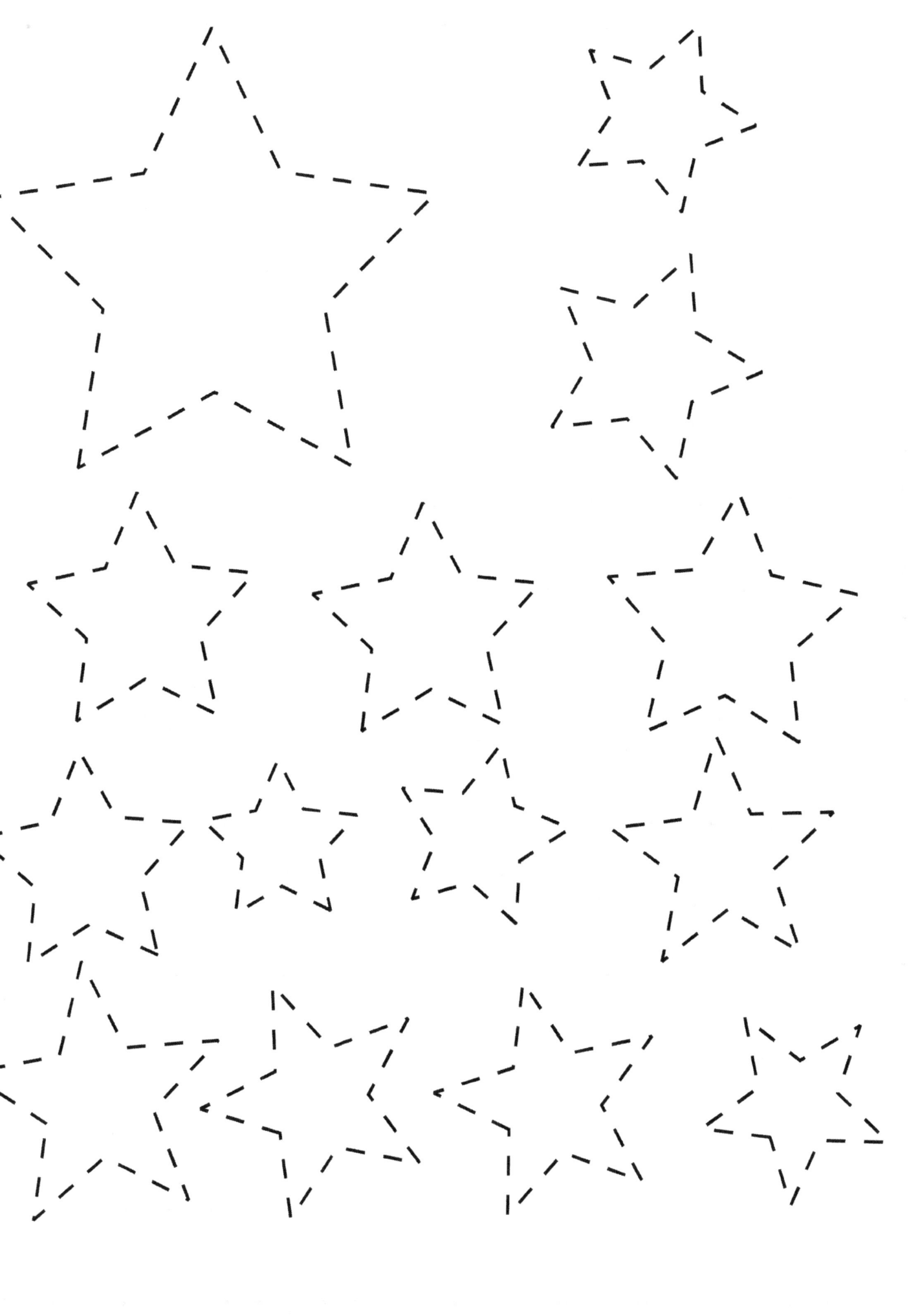

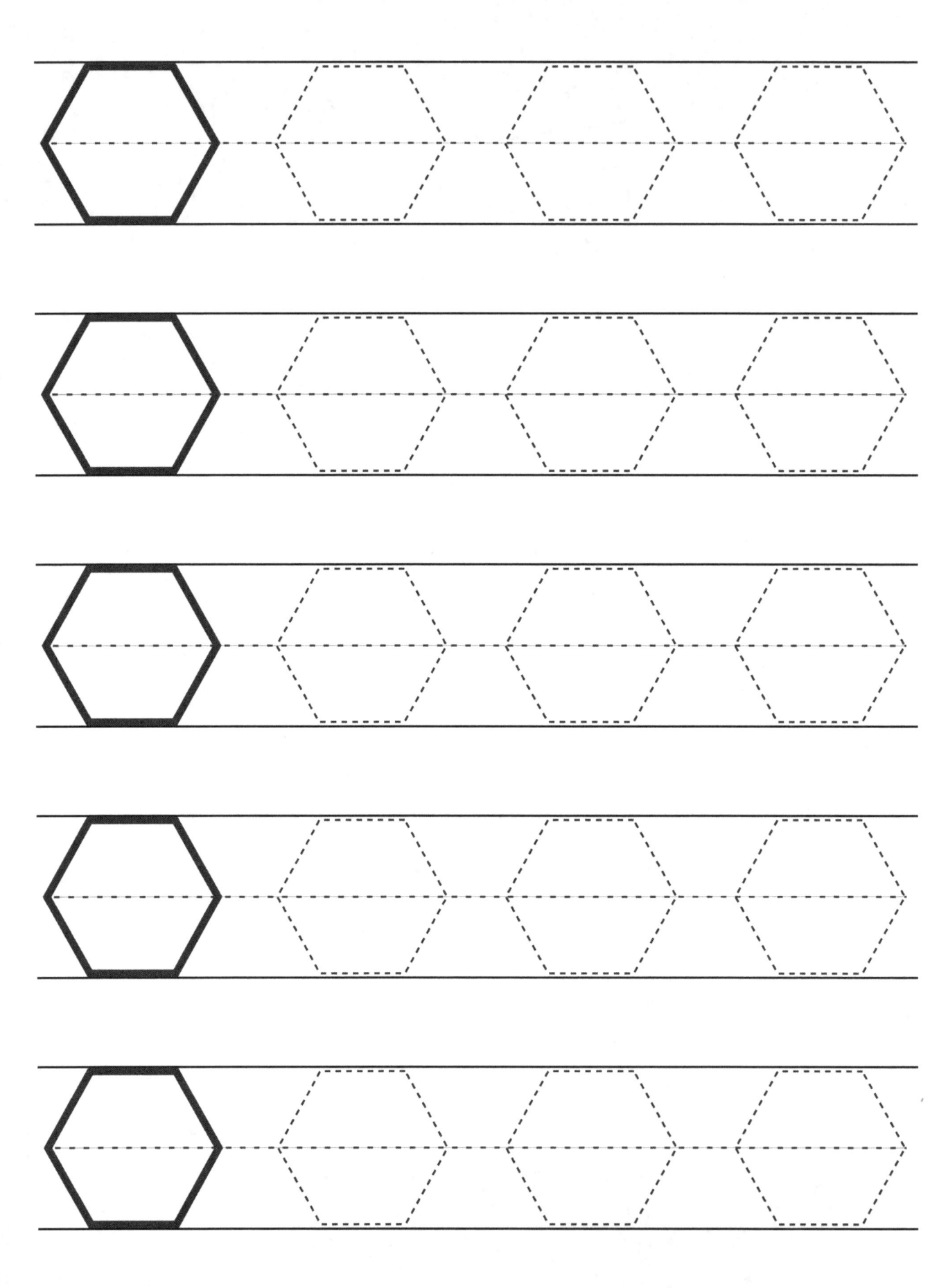

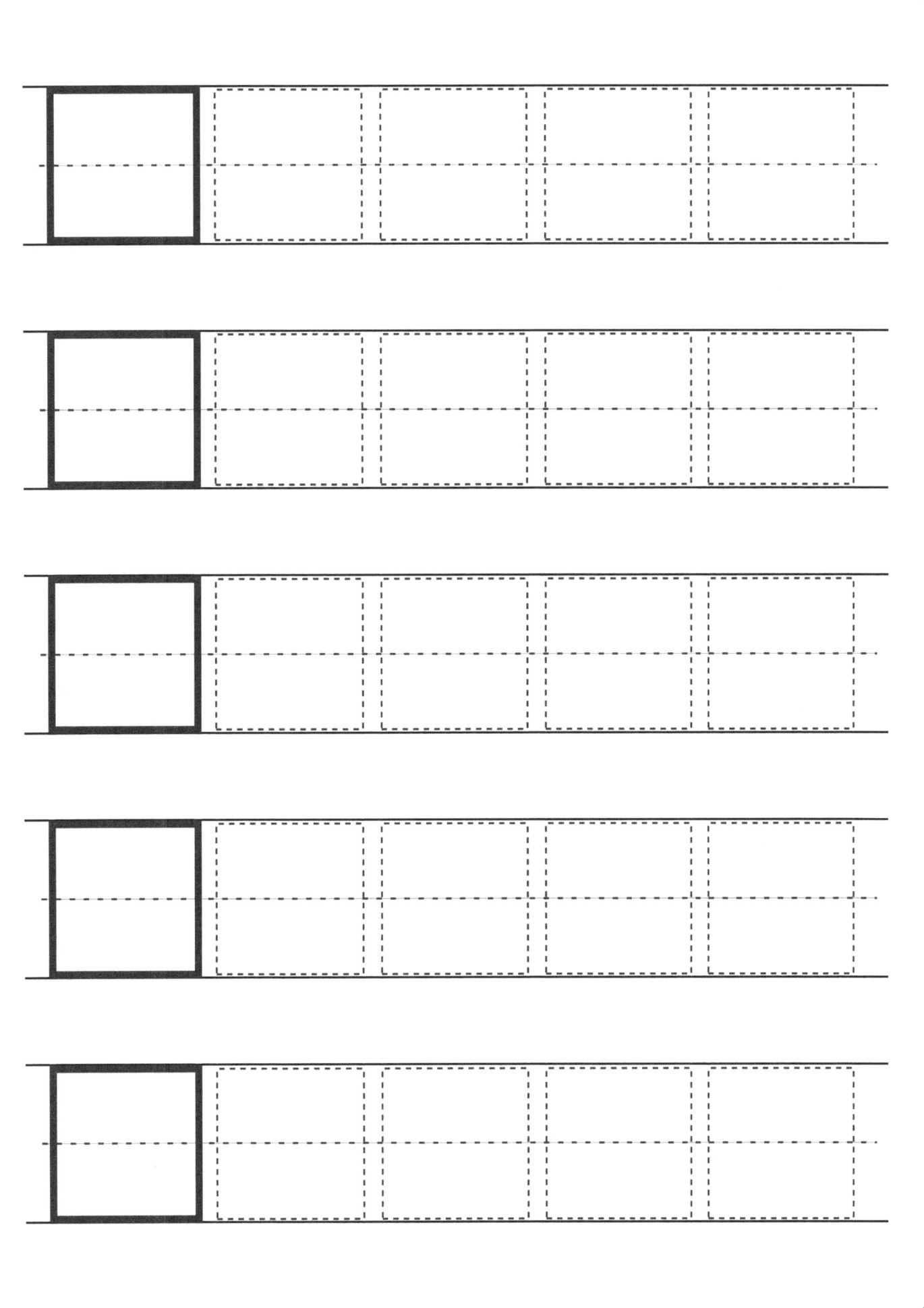

Check out my other book

www.ingramcontent.com/pod-product-compliance
Lightning Source LLC
Chambersburg PA
CBHW080956120626
46546CB00010B/2910